Entrance to Churchyard, Chalfont St. Giles

Particular Places

An introduction to English local history

Christopher Lewis

The British Library

This book accompanies the exhibition *Particular Places:
English local history and the Victoria County History* which opened
in April 1989 in the British Library galleries, sponsored by the
Landmark Trust.

Grateful acknowledgement is made to the following for permission
to reproduce illustrations which are their copyright: Mr A. P. Baggs
(9), Cambridgeshire Collection at Cambridge City Library
(Cambridgeshire County Council) (23), Crown copyright/RAF
(13), Public Record Office (Crown copyright material by
permission of the Controller of Her Majesty's Stationery Office)
(h), Royal Commission on the Historical Monuments of England
(4, 17), Tewkesbury town council (Plate 6), Vestry House Museum
(London Borough of Waltham Forest) (c, d), Mr A. P. Wakelin (a).

The engravings on pp.1, 2, 11, 19, 29, 35, 43, 53, and 65 are taken
from VCH volumes published between 1904 and 1925. The seal
on p.2 is from the borough of Scarborough.

First published 1989 by
The British Library
Great Russell Street, London WC1B 3DG

British Library Cataloguing in Publication Data
Lewis, Christopher
  Particular places: an introduction to
  English local history
  1. England. Local history
  I. Title
  942

ISBN 0 7123 0175 5

Designed by Alan Bartram
Typeset and Printed in England by
BAS Printers Limited, Over Wallop, Stockbridge, Hampshire

Contents

Burial register of St Leonard's parish, Colchester
See p.18.
BL Add. MS 60257, f.1

Burialls 1664

July
Samuell Son of John Robby and Jone
was buried y 16th day

August
Elizabethe wife of goodman Chapman was buried
the 19th day
Thomas sonne of G. Crosman was buried
the same day
Charles sonne of John Rutin and Esse was
buried the 20th day

September
the wyfe of Stephen King was buried y
13th day.

October
Sara wife of Benjamin Burnatt was
buried the first day.

November
Francis Harby buried y 5th day.

December
Rebeca wyfe of John Reynoles buried 6 day

January
Elizabeth wyfe of John freeman buried y 13
Susan Clamp widdow y 17 day buried
the wyfe of goodman Sewel also buried 17 day
John Sewel buried y 24th day
John Smith an apprentice ... buried y 28

March
William Page buried y 7 day

May
Thomas son of Stephen King & Elizabeth buried y 12 day

June
William mullines buried y 14 day
John flore buried y 18 day
Elizabeth Reynoles buried y 23 day

Septemb
Priscilla y wife of goodm Smith
Jane wyfe of John Foster
The widdow Preston
James hamon

Octob
Mary Hammon
The wyfe of Godm Oxbury
Three Children of William Tittle

Novemb
Elizabeth wyfe of william Tittle
Henry summer son
Joseph. Nathaniel Doweish

13635

Preface

Among the various avenues of historical study, local history has the advantage and merit of being unusually accessible to the amateur and to the general public. However scholarly, academic, or technical some of the approaches to local history may be, the non-expert student is able not only to read the subject with pleasure but also, without too long an apprenticeship or formidable qualifications, to join the research and writing. Partly that is because everybody comes from, lives in, and belongs to a particular place.

This book is produced in connection with an exhibition to mark the publication of 200 volumes of the Victoria County History, an encyclopaedia of English local history which, for the places that it has covered, provides an outline of the essential facts and references and an indispensable starting point for further inquiry. The author of this book, a member of the editorial staff of the VCH, tells how to pursue such inquiry, at several different levels, whether or not the relevant volume of the VCH has already been published.

The help of the following people in the preparation of the book is gratefully acknowledged: Andrew Prescott, David Way, and Anne Young of the British Library; Xanthe Brooke, Audrey Coney, John Evans (Waltham Forest Archives), Robert Peberdy, and Peter Wakelin (Portbooks Programme, Wolverhampton Polytechnic).

CHRISTOPHER ELRINGTON
General Editor, Victoria County History

Introduction

This book has been written as an appetiser for anyone interested in the history of a particular place who has not done any systematic research. It is also for those who have made a beginning and want to know more about other aspects of English local history. If an individual town, city, village, suburb, county, or some other region has struck you as having an interesting past, or if you have thought of finding out about the history of your own family, this book will outline the shape of English local history as a whole, pointing out the different places at which it is possible to start and where they lie in relation to one another. It is an aerial view of the subject which can be supplemented by reference to books giving more detailed information on topics and sources.

Local history is not something separate from history in general, though it appears to many people quite different from the subject taught in most schools until recently. All history is about people. Local historians, who concentrate on individual towns and villages, spend most of their time investigating ordinary people in ordinary places. The ordinariness is one of the attractions. Another is that local historians use many documents which have hardly been examined for their historical interest. All local historians make new findings about the places which they research; W. G. Hoskins once claimed that on average he made one major discovery a week.

It is not necessary to define the nature of local history in order to enjoy doing it or to produce worthwhile results, but it deserves some thought. Local history has grown quickly over the past 30 or 40 years and there is no sign that interest is slackening. More people are interested and active in research than ever before. There are more societies, more publications, and a widening range of topics with which local historians are concerned. New specialisations such as family history, industrial archaeology, landscape history, and urban history, all once recognisably part of local history, threaten to become completely separate subjects. The empire of local history is in decay and it is time to rally round its flag.

Some practitioners feel that there is a distinction between 'professionals', employed full-time as teachers in higher education or in libraries or record offices, and 'amateurs' working in their own time. Anyone who has read much local history will know that it is a distinction without a difference. The only difference that matters is that between good and bad local history; the ability to do thorough research, answer interesting questions, and write well has nothing at all to do with whether you are a 'professional' or an 'amateur', a full-timer or a part-timer.

Full-time local historians in higher education are naturally more introspective about the future of the subject than part-timers: after all, their livelihood and academic standing depend on whether local history has a future or not. They constantly feel the need to look around the subject and take stock. Articles and pamphlets appear

God blesseth trewe labour / with plentye and fauour. Be still quicke and kinde / Reward thou shalt finde.

2

At the Generall Quarter Sessions of the peace held
by adjournm[en]t at Wigan in and for the county
palatine of Lancaster the Sixteenth day of January
in the Eleventh year of King George the seconds
Reign.

26

The order made by John Plumb and William Hill —
Esquires Two of his Ma[jes]ties Justices of the peace and
Quorum in and for the County of Lancaster under their
hands and seals bearing date the Third day of January
last for the removall of William Lin and Martha his wife
Alice John and Robert their Children out of Skelmersdale
poor persons
into Chorley both in the said county and for settlem[en]t
of them in Chorley aforesaid is by this Court upon the —
Appeal of the Inhabitants of Chorley aforesaid and on full
hearing of both the said Towns ratifyed and confirmed

Ravald

3

These woole horse and other
first of husbandry

Item of ... d ...
Item of wante whyt and black ...
Item of horse harnes my parcel ...
Item in yacks pryce ...
Item ...
...

4

Pewte brasse and other

5

PLATE 2
Ordinance Book of the Bakers' Company of York

The bakers' guild in Tudor York was numerous, wealthy, and powerful, but was strictly supervised by the city council to ensure regular and reasonably priced supplies of bread. In the mid 15th century, the city temporarily broke the guild's monopoly, restoring it only on condition of lower prices. Eight drawings of bakers at work, here shaping and cutting dough, enliven a collection of guild orders made in 1596. At the bottom of the page is written
Who so followethe theis preceptes well,
In heaven shall have a place to dwell.
BL Add. MS 34605, f.25

PLATE 3
Poor-law removal order

The Lancashire magistrates, sitting in Quarter Sessions at Wigan on 16 January 1738, here order the removal of William Livock, his wife Martha, and their children Alice, John, and Robert from Skelmersdale in Ormskirk parish to Chorley some 12 miles away. Under the Poor Relief Act of 1662, everyone had a legal place of 'settlement' in a parish or township which was obliged to support them in poverty. The Livocks were legally settled in Chorley, and Skelmersdale had no duty to relieve them.
BL Add. MS 36876, f.26

PLATE 4
A farmer's inventory from Stockton, Wiltshire

Inventories of farmers' goods drawn up when their wills were proved are an important source for agricultural history. Thomas Toppe's inventory, dated 1560, reflects the business of a rich farmer in the Chalk country of Wiltshire (**19**). Headings for 'catall' and 'corne and hay' are followed by this for 'chese, woole, horse and other stuff of husbandry'. The thirteenth item is 'a wynnyng shete' (a sheet to winnow threshed corn), followed by '2 busshills to mett corne' (bushel measures for corn)

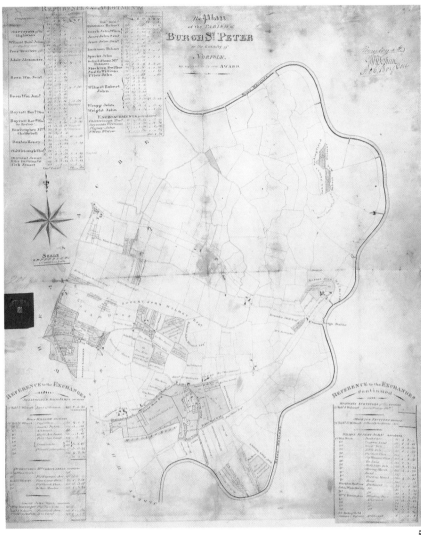

and '56 flytches of bacon', probably for sale.
BL Add. Roll 59152

PLATE 5
Inclosure map of Burgh St Peter, Norfolk

An inclosure act was passed for Burgh St Peter in 1811. Unlike that for Widmerpool (**24**), it dealt with only a small part of the parish, the 130 acres of commons and greens (coloured green). The arable land was already long inclosed, as the map shows. The opportunity was also taken to rationalise scattered land holdings by a series of exchanges (coloured yellow). The map was drawn to accompany the formal award of land.
BL Egerton MS 3162

5

PLATE 6
Tewkesbury Quay, 1804
Barges are shown being loaded with goods traded in the town, including casks which may contain cider, sacks of salt from Droitwich, and sacks of barley and malt. Coal stacked on the quay was partly for use in malthouses. A three-legged steelyard is being used to weigh coal before it is carried into town. Beyond the quay can be seen boat builders, and fishing nets hung to dry. Barges and larger two-masted trows (shown on the right) were sailed or hauled (as on the far bank) from Tewkesbury down into the Bristol Channel and far upstream into Warwickshire and Shropshire.
Pen-and-wash drawing at Tewkesbury town hall, photograph by Posers Photographic Studio

from time to time pushing one definition as against another, pressing or denying the claims of regional history as a successor to local history, and sometimes even declaring that local history is dead and recommending that we all go back to studying kings and parliaments. All points of view except the last have something to be said in their favour. Such introspective musings have not been very enlightening for the great majority of local historians, largely because they have failed to see local history as a whole in all its diversity.

There are several assumptions behind this book. Some of them stem from the fact that the author works for what is known formally as the Victoria History of the Counties of England and to all local historians as the VCH. It is, nevertheless, a personal and not an official view of what local history is about. The VCH's method, explained more fully in the final chapter, is to write the local history of England place by place, taking each parish or town in turn and trying to deal comprehensively with each, with a parallel treatment at county level of certain wider topics. Working for the VCH has given me two fundamental beliefs about local history. The first is that everywhere has an interesting past, even places that a non-local historian might see as the dullest suburb of a dreary town or the most woebegone hamlet in a dismal county. The second is that the drier and more 'old-fashioned' parts of local history, notably descents of manors and institutional histories of parish churches and charities, are no less essential to understanding an individual place than more glamorous and fashionable topics like demography and landscape.

It so happens that the VCH's 'one place at a time' approach matches the interests of most part-timers, who themselves either take one place at a time or, more commonly, limit themselves to one place altogether. Most people are drawn to the subject precisely because they are interested in one particular place, though they need not and usually do not try to study it in its entirety.

A generous and sensible definition might be that English local history covers every conceivable subject which can be studied within a geographical area smaller than the country as a whole. It includes everything from individual families and buildings to major regions of England over lengthy periods of time and comprehends all the specialisms which it has encouraged in recent years. It is distinguished from national history by the fact that the individual locality comes first. There is a world of difference between the national historian, almost always a full-time professional, who raids local sources to cast light on the general problems of English history, and the local historian for whom one particular place is paramount. The special character of local history is not that it is something less complex than national history and easier to do; if anything the reverse is true. What best defines local history as a separate subject eminently suitable for part-time study is that it is the story of people in small social groups living in one place rather than another.

I have tried to write mainly with part-timers in mind, whether they are newcomers to local history or have some experience. For those who have never done any research there are some ideas about what topics can be undertaken and some suggestions on what to do next, and especially what more detailed guides to read (*see* Further Reading, p.77, where the local studies mentioned in passing are also listed). The book is intended to show how the different parts of the subject – family history, parish history, urban history, and regional history – fit together as a whole and why at the core of what local historians do is the history of particular places.

CHRISTOPHER LEWIS

Family History

Hesketh of Rufford   Towneley of Towneley   Farrer of Hall Garth

Local history begins at home. The first impulse for many local historians is a primitive urge to know where they came from or what sort of people lived in their house before them. It begins with such simple questions as 'How old is my house?' and 'Who were my great-grandparents?' Most of the answers are quite easily found. For family history in the 19th and 20th centuries, there are no special skills to be mastered except a methodical approach and persistence. Houses put up in the 19th and 20th centuries usually present no great difficulties, while those from before the era of mass-produced building materials can be tackled with the help of John H. Harvey's *Sources for the History of Houses*, written for the 'amateur beginner'. With a little experience you will be able to discover the identity of anyone's great-grandparents and at least something about any house. There is some straightforward advice on how to get started on the history of a house or a family later in this book (*see* pp.66-7, 70-1).

Although the histories of families and houses seem to belong naturally together, they will normally be pursued in isolation. Only in the most aristocratic families, and even then only among a small minority, has one family owned (let alone inhabited) one house for more than a few generations. One of those upper-class exceptions is examined in a little detail later. Ordinary working people in town and country moved from house to house with a frequency which is irritating if they happen to have been your own elusive ancestors. Moreover, the demolition of older houses has been so extensive that there will be a good chance that even the houses where a generation as recent as your grandparents were born are no longer standing. The history of houses is largely ignored in the rest of this chapter: it is much less appealing for most people for the good reason that most people's houses are rather less interesting than their families. On the other hand, the basic techniques for finding out about individual houses should be learnt by all genealogists. A knowledge of where and how your ancestors lived adds much to the enjoyment and understanding of their history.

The simplest questions about a house or a family will immediately draw the curious back into a wider consideration of their own personal past. The first set of answers becomes a point of departure for new questions. What was here before the house was built? Who were my grandparents' parents? Novice researchers will soon see that their own inquiry opens up many questions about the history of one or more places. Why was this side of the road built up before the other? Why did great-grandfather leave the village where his father and grandfather had lived and move to the town? Such questions which arise naturally out of the history of families cannot be answered without considering wider matters. Individual families and houses are the building blocks which form larger local communities, and the study of them is inseparable from at least some consideration of the local setting. The sort of evidence which is used for family history, apart from the most basic of all – certificates of births, marriages, and deaths – relates to a community in a particular place and not just to the individuals who are the object of the immediate inquiry. A census book for 1881, examined in order to find the family of an ancestor known to have been born in a particular house later in the decade, allows you to look inside every house in the street. Which families could afford servants? Which were taking in lodgers? Had widowed parents moved in with their married children? Which children of a growing family were still living at home? Had the older ones followed their father's trade? Had the family moved about the country so that the children were all born in different places, or were they long settled in one place? Anyone with an average amount of curiosity about people cannot fail to be fascinated by the mid 19th-century censuses. It is the same with directories, which from the mid 19th century until the Second World War or later listed the farmers and tradesmen of every village (though not the majority of people) and in the larger towns gave a detailed account of householders, shopkeepers, and businesses (1). Comparing a detailed town directory with an Ordnance Survey map on a scale large enough to distinguish individual houses is an absorbing task, particularly if you know the place as it is now, with all the changes that have taken place. Curiosity about ordinary people and ordinary places in the past is at the heart of local history and forms a natural link between families and localities.

The history of a single family or house can legitimately be an end in itself and should not be belittled by those whose historical interests are wider. Both are well-defined topics, large enough to involve the use of a surprising variety of sources but at the same time sufficiently narrow to be completed within a limited amount of time. Their limits should be recognised: in themselves, if carried no further, they will not be of much general interest beyond other family members or those who have known or lived in the house. In the rare cases where a family had local influence, its story may well modify the accepted picture of local society, while the history of an individual house may, likewise, occasionally have something of interest to say about the development of the area in which it stands. For the most part, however, historians of ordinary houses and ordinary families cannot expect to make much impact on what is known about even a single village or town.

1 Colchester in 1910

The firm of Benham & Co regularly published a directory for Colchester and district between 1881 and 1965. Streets are listed alphabetically, as are occupiers' names in each street. Though inconvenient for some research purposes, this arrangement makes a search for an individual living in Colchester whose address is unknown easier than the more normal house-by-house listings.
BL Printed Books, PP.2507.ch, 1910 edn, p.123

```
16 Paxman, J. N.              Stores                    21 Rogers, H. G.
46 Perry, G.            Colin  Taylor,   King,          15 Sorsbie, Mrs.
49 Pilgrim, D.             and Co.                      30 Wallace, R. W.
82 Pilgrim, D. W.       26 Cracknell, R.                10 Young, Col. H. H.
108 Pilgrim, G. S.      11 Denny, A. F.
143 Pike, H. S.            Gas Works                    IPSWICH ROAD.
65 Potter, A.           23 Hales, D.
55 Powell, W.           4 and 5 Jarvis and Hibbs          Ackers, H. G., Supt.,
123 Presnall, E. H., post  9 Jarvis, W. S.                 county police station
     office             22 Kent, B.                     60 Barrell, A. W.
13 Priddy, A. S.           Littlebury and Son           60 Barrell, W.
71 Raper, H.               London, J. M., Anchor        25 Barrett, A.
138 Rayner, A.                Inn                        13 Bedwell, M.
10 Rayner, E. C.        28 Moy, T., Ltd.                32 Bedwell, M.
72 Rayner, J.              Noy, B.                       21 Biggs, Mrs.
61 Richer, W. E.        8 and 13 Owen, Parry,              Bowley, M., New
18 Rigg, J.                and Co.                           Cottages
17 Rigg, W. L.          2 Pertwee, F.                   27 Buckler, —
90 Rogers, F. W.        4 Radcliffe, H.                 36 Burgess, A.
84 Rooke, W. A.         10 Sharp, Miss                     Colchester Steam
140 Sargeant, G.           Taylor,  G.,  The New             Laundry Co.
131 Scott, J. W.              Dock Inn                      Cook, Mrs. E.
117 Scott, R.           2 Truman and Hanbury               Cottee, J.
41 SHEPHARD & SON,      1 Wright, F.                    26 Day, F.
   Undertakers and      14 YOUNGS,     J.   H.,         58 Deeks, J.
   Funeral    Fur-         The  Neptune.                40 Duckett, W.
   nishers                 Daniell's    ales,           16 Dyer, C. W.
47 Smith, A. P.            stout, wines, and               Edwards,   E.,   police
122 Snowden, J.            spirits                           station
126 SOUTHGATE, J. E.,                                      Fisher, J. D., Rovers'
   The  Dolphin,        HYTHE STATION RD                     Tye Farm
   Daniell's   ales,    23 Bateman, —                    14 Gay, A.
   stout, wines and     25 Beckwith, G. E.              5 Golding, Miss
   spirits                 Brackett,  F.  W.,  and      6 Halls, R.
7 Stebbing, A. J.          Co., Ltd.                    2 Harden, W.
```

Family history has contributed to national history in other ways. The great advances which have recently been made in understanding the growth of the population of England in the 17th and 18th centuries have been achieved by accumulating an enormous number of outline histories of individual families, focusing in particular on crucial aspects such as age at marriage and the number of children who survived to have children of their own. The scale of such a project means that historians of an individual family or even of the 16 converging families of their great-great-grandparents can contribute relatively little to a national picture.

Family historians go about their task in a variety of ways, since there are probably almost as many different ideas of who counts as a family member as there are individuals. Nevertheless, two basic approaches to the history of families can be distinguished, traditional and popular.

Traditional family history

The traditional approach to the history of a family imitates that of the genealogists who from the 16th century, if not earlier, traced the landowning families of England down the generations. They produced some 'family histories' of striking appearance (PLATE 1). Because manors and other landed estates passed by primogeniture, genealogy was essentially the story of individual lineages bearing the same surname, as the layout of a family tree indicates. When tracing a family forward in time, as traditional family history does, it can be virtually impossible to follow up a married daughter unless she was the heir.

The sources for the traditional family history of landed families and their estates always allowed and indeed encouraged the historian to follow them forward in this way, tracing each stage at which ownership of an estate passed from one person to another. They were really the histories of individual pieces of landed property, which might at one extreme belong to a single family for generations and so serve as outline genealogies, or at the other extreme have passed by a continuous series of sales from individual to individual. In practice, most manors not in the hands of institutions descended by a mixture of inheritance and sale, so overlapping at different periods with the histories of several landed families.

Most families of gentry status have at least an outline account of their history somewhere in print, or a great abundance of material for constructing one. Commonly there will be a 'descent' of the family under its principal residence in the Victoria County History (if written) or one of the older county histories. On the other hand, a family comprises rather more people than a succession of eldest sons or other heirs. Wives, daughters, and younger sons will all be considered in a true gentry family history, as opposed to an account of their lands. Where there is an existing account of a landowning family in the form of one or more estate histories, the local historian who wishes to write such a history can use that as a starting point. Because of the supreme influence of landowning families over local affairs, a history of such a family can, if properly constructed, be very illuminating about local conditions in the past.

The method of tracing landed families, brought to a fine art in the early volumes of the VCH, remains of central importance in the study of English local history because of the enduring importance of the structure and character of land ownership in rural society. It extends to urban history in the 19th century when the pace and direction of the growth of suburbs was determined first and foremost by landowners. H. J. Dyos's pioneering study *Victorian Suburb*, for example, delineated the process for Camberwell in south London.

The methods of traditional family history are still appropriate if pursuing a landowning family. An examination of any of the VCH's 'topographical' volumes shows the range of sources to be used and the type of information which can be extracted from them. Tracing manors and manorial families is one of the more difficult technical accomplishments of the local historian and something which the genealogist intent on pursuing a landed family will need to acquire. An example from one of the first counties to be completed by the VCH illustrates some of the points.

William Farrer's history of the Hesketh family of Rufford for the Victoria History of Lancashire was based in the first place on prodigiously wide research among published and unpublished sources. His transcripts of original documents, now in Manchester Central Library, are voluminous. Farrer and John Brownbill went systematically

2 The Towneley transcripts

Christopher Towneley (1604-74) spent a lifetime transcribing old documents owned by Lancashire gentry families for a projected history of the county, among them those of the Heskeths of Rufford, to whom he was related by marriage. As he wrote in the heading to the Hesketh section, 'These deeds following I had of John Molineux of Rufforth Esqr the twenty fift day of June Anno Domini 1661'. The first two deeds which he copied dated from 1528 and 1534 and related to land in Wrightington and Parbold, near Rufford.
BL Add. MS 32107, f.143v

through the appropriate classes in the Public Record Office and the indexes of the British Library's (then British Museum's) manuscript collections in London. They sought out the transcripts made by earlier Lancashire historians and antiquarians such as the 17th-century Christopher Towneley, who had seen and copied many documents afterwards lost (2), and went through the muniment rooms of landed families in the county, including that of the Heskeths.

Among the more useful types of document for manorial families

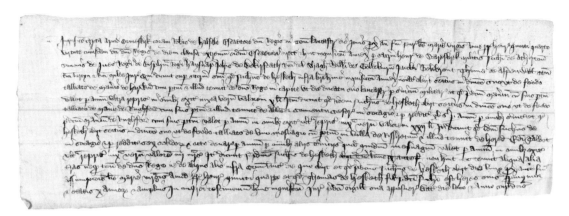

3 Inquisition *post mortem* on Nicholas Hesketh, 1417
The abbreviated Latin of the final two and a half lines gives the information that Nicholas Hesketh died on 10 August 1416 and that his heir was his son Thomas, aged 10. The hearing which established the facts and recorded Nicholas's landholdings, including the manor of Rufford (*Rughford*, line 7, 5th word), was held at Ormskirk on 28 January 1417 (line 1). The document was borrowed from official custody at Lancaster by Christopher Towneley (2) in 1659 and was perhaps never returned, since it found its way into the hands of the Norris family and eventually to the British Library. BL Add. Charter 51558

are inquisitions *post mortem*, drawn up at the instance of the Crown on the death of an important landowner in order to ensure that the Crown continued to receive the obligations due from his successor. The genealogical information which can be extracted comprises the date of a man's death and the name, family relationship, and age of his heir (3). Manorial history is much harder to write after the time when inquisitions were abolished, formally in 1660 and in practice during the Civil War in the 1640s.

The Heskeths owned Rufford and used it as their main residence for a particularly long time. The chronicler of the family must therefore take into account the family's houses at Rufford, the Old Hall and the New Hall, the first of which is now owned by the National Trust and has a complex history inseparable from the family story. Much about the Old Hall can be linked directly with the lives and aspirations of individual members of the Hesketh family (4).

The new family history

The traditional approach to genealogy exemplified by the VCH's account of the Heskeths is not appropriate at all for ordinary families. Fortunately, for a variety of reasons, family history has undergone a popular and democratic revolution in recent years. Certificates of births, marriages, and deaths, which form the starting point for those tracing a family history, have always been open to public inspection, but their usefulness was restricted until mid 19th-century censuses and earlier parish registers became available. In both cases, access has been transformed since the 1950s. Because the census enumerators' books are closed for 100 years after compilation, and because the 1851 census books are the first to include information useful to the family historian (precise ages and birth places, occupations, and relationships to the head of the household), it was not until the 1950s that historians of ordinary families could exploit a rich store of information. As each successive decennial census becomes available in the future, beginning with the 1891 census in 1992, and as the task of compiling street

4 Rufford Old Hall, Lancashire
The timber-framed great hall (right),
with a bay window to light the high
table, is the only surviving part of a
15th-century house built probably
by Thomas or Robert Hesketh, son
and grandson of Nicholas Hesketh of
(3). The east wing (left) was rebuilt
for another Thomas Hesketh, whose
initials are over the doorway with a
datestone of 1662. The timber-
framed gabled block between the two
wings (centre) was altered in 1821,
when the house was repaired to ac-
commodate the eldest son of the
Hesketh family. The head of the
family by then lived at Rufford New
Hall.
National Monuments Record, AA
51/3245

indexes to towns and cities proceeds, so an ever greater bulk of
detailed information for family historians will become available.

Parallel with the progressive opening of the censuses has been the
concentration of parish registers in county record offices since the
Second World War. It has been a cumulative process, not quite complete, and accessibility has been further improved by the efforts of
selfless individuals who transcribe and index the registers and collate
them with the parallel series of 'bishop's transcripts'. For family
historians who have been methodical, persistent, and lucky enough
to push their search back to the early 19th century or before, that
alone has made the rapid and efficient search for ancestors a realistic
proposition. Before, it was necessary to read the original unindexed
registers one by one in a succession of damp and draughty church
vestries.

Despite the transformation of family history, some people remain
determined to push back the story of their family in one single line
from generation to generation as far as possible, from certificates of
births, marriages, and deaths and census returns to parish registers
(5) and ultimately to the varied medieval records which name and list
individuals. For most families the aim is unrealistic, which avoids the
more awkward question of whether it is worth doing at all. Except
for landed families it will be virtually impossible to prove a succession
of links to take the family back much before 1600 and in many cases
research will break down considerably nearer the present day.

The ability to track down ever-receding generations of a single line
is a technique of family history rather than family history itself. For
one thing, there is the question of deciding which line to pursue.
Some guides to genealogy declare a preference for pursuing one
surname on the grounds that it makes research easier. While it may
be interesting to track down the details of your father's father's
father's father's father, he will not necessarily be a more interesting
person, historically, than your mother's mother's mother's mother's
mother, or indeed any other of the 32 members of that generation.
Tracing a succession of fathers and sons, or mothers and daughters,

should not be confused with the history of a family as a whole. We do not today regard only our fathers and our eldest sons as 'family', and nor did people in the past.

A more profitable approach to the individual family has been advocated in a recent book by David Hey, *Family History and Local History in England*, written for family historians who want to go beyond collecting names and dates to consider the communities in which their ancestors lived. He suggests as a first objective identifying 16 great-great-grandparents, which is realistic technically since it does not normally involve the use of any particularly difficult or inaccessible sources. As a starting point for tracing the family forward in time to the present day it has the added interest of providing contrasts in occupations and places of residence among the different branches of the family. The 16 names gathered can alternatively, or later, be the starting point for pushing some lines (the more interesting or the easiest) further back.

Even those who start genealogical research with the narrowest of objectives should find themselves drawn into the many byways of family history. Occupations, changing place of residence, choice of marriage partners, number of children, life expectancy, even choice of forenames are all subjects on which the researcher will turn up evidence and which form part of the rich context that turns genealogy from ancestor worship into the study of a family or families in society. In some ways family history is the most fundamental sort of social history. Once the techniques of discovering information about people and their family relationships in the past have been understood, it seems a pity to waste them on trying to turn up some noble forebear.

5 Burial register of St Leonard's parish, Colchester
Registers of baptisms, marriages, and burials were kept from 1538, though few early ones survive. Colchester was ravaged by plague and smallpox in 1665 and 1666. The three children and wife of William Tittle, buried in October and November 1665 (third and fourth entries from end) were probably victims of one or the other. St Leonard's parish, which lay one mile east of Colchester, seems to have avoided the worst of the double epidemic. Altogether perhaps 2,000 people died in the town, at least a quarter of the population (*see* p. 6 for complete document).
BL Add. MS 60257, f.1

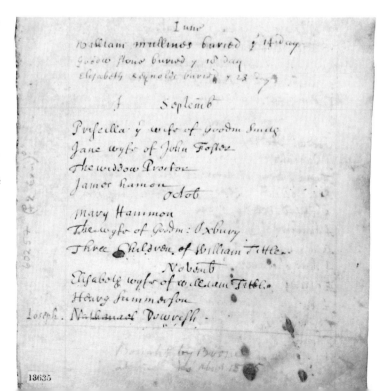

Parish History

UPPER RAWCLIFFE : ST. MICHAEL'S VILLAGE

The history of individual places, or topography, is going out of fashion in some quarters as the claims of regional historians and the narrower objectives of genealogists compete with it for precedence. Yet 'particular places' have always been the backbone of English local history, and the reason for the great surge of popular interest in recent years has been precisely because newly available sources and new approaches to the subject have made the histories of individual towns and villages all over the country accessible and interesting to their inhabitants. The small-scale local study of a village, a parish, or a small town remains the typical local history. Its validity as a form of historical inquiry deserves emphasis in view of the tendency of some local historians to take a narrower or wider angle of vision. This chapter therefore examines the character of local history as the story of individual rural places, leaving urban history for separate treatment. The idea of 'parish history' has some unfortunate connotations bound up with the bad old antiquarian past of local history and the fact that the term 'parochial' came in the 19th century to have derogatory overtones; but it is unavoidable. All it means in this context is the history of individual rural places. Not all of them were parishes even when the term is loosely defined.

Two preliminary observations are necessary about the relationship of genealogy and regional history to topography. First, genealogists for the most part do not pursue merely the names and dates of their ancestors but their identities. Family history cannot be done in a satisfying or meaningful way by an intelligent researcher if it does not take account of the places in which members of a family lived. At the other end of the spectrum, regional history makes no sense if divorced from individual places within the region. Similarly, those interested in individual buildings or businesses or local institutions should be aware of the places in which they were located in order to understand them. Almost all historians need to know in some detail about the history of individual places.

The history of everywhere in England has not yet been written, so family historians, regional historians, and others with special interests will not necessarily find a satisfactory account of an individual place in which they are interested. National coverage is uneven, despite the existence of 200 volumes of the Victoria County History and the fact that there can hardly be a place in the country for which there is not some published work of local history, be it the VCH, an older county history, a local publication, or antiquarian jottings. There is a great deal to be done in writing outline accounts of parishes and towns. This is not to suggest that genealogists and regional historians should stop what they are doing in order to write about individual places. The point is simply that all local historians, whatever their precise interests, need to understand the special character of particular places, and that sometimes they will have to do the work themselves.

Most topographers start with a single special place and often, quite reasonably, proceed no further. It can be a lifetime's work and more to know the history of even a single small village really thoroughly. At the academic level too, local historians commonly write about the places or districts to which they have a special attachment. Even historians who use local studies mainly to shed light on problems of national history may find it difficult, given the sheer diversity of English local history, to select places to study on purely objective criteria. The strong attachment of local historians to particular localities is a strength rather than an admission of subjectivity. The very best local historians have always written most vividly about the places to which their heart belongs. To read W. G. Hoskins's opening words in a pioneering article about deserted medieval villages is to see how the love of a particular landscape can sharpen critical understanding of its history: 'As the sun sets behind the crumpled outline of the Charnwood Hills, the evening light throws long shadows across the pastures of east and south Leicestershire, revealing in many places the presence of shallow ditches and banks that form a distinct pattern'.*

Transactions of the Leicestershire Archaeological Society, 22 (1946), p.241.

Parishes and townships

For most of history, most people in England have lived by agriculture or related trades in small communities in the countryside. Ask the English about the lives of their ancestors and they will think of farmers and labourers, country blacksmiths and village shopkeepers. Villages were important but were never the only form of rural settlement, and the popular image of a typical village with church and manor house was even rarer. There were some with many manors and some with more than one church, while both manors and parishes commonly covered more than one village, so leaving some villages

6 Thirty-one parishes in south-east Cambridgeshire

By late Anglo-Saxon times, the densely settled population of Cambridgeshire was served by churches rarely more than two miles apart. Parishes were consequently small. Those in the western part of the area shown normally contained a single village, those in the wooded east had scattered farms and hamlets. Two oddities not shown on this map are that Fulbourn (3) and Duxford (21) each comprised two parishes, while Bartlow (28) extended over the county boundary into Essex. Otherwise the pattern is very regular.

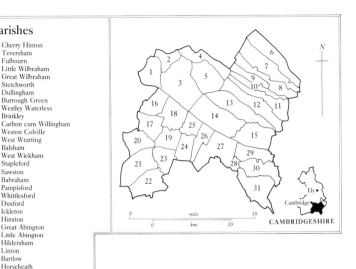

Parishes

1 Cherry Hinton
2 Teversham
3 Fulbourn
4 Little Wilbraham
5 Great Wilbraham
6 Stetchworth
7 Dullingham
8 Burrough Green
9 Westley Waterless
10 Brinkley
11 Carlton cum Willingham
12 Weston Colville
13 West Wratting
14 Balsham
15 West Wickham
16 Stapleford
17 Sawston
18 Babraham
19 Pampisford
20 Whittlesford
21 Duxford
22 Ickleton
23 Hinxton
24 Great Abington
25 Little Abington
26 Hildersham
27 Linton
28 Bartlow
29 Horseheath
30 Shudy Camps
31 Castle Camps

CAMBRIDGESHIRE

7 One parish in north-east Lancashire

An enormous, sparsely populated area of north-east Lancashire, covering over 100,000 acres, was originally served from a single minster (collegiate) church at Whalley (1). By the 12th century, at the latest, dependent chapels without full parochial rights had been established in certain places, and new chapelries continued to be created until the 18th century. In the early modern period, the townships undertook the functions managed in Cambridgeshire by parishes. The extra-parochial townships were nominally attached to the church of St Mary in Clitheroe castle (40).

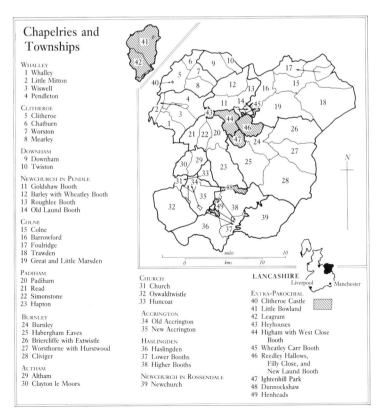

Chapelries and Townships

WHALLEY
1 Whalley
2 Little Mitton
3 Wiswell
4 Pendleton

CLITHEROE
5 Clitheroe
6 Chatburn
7 Worston
8 Mearley

DOWNHAM
9 Downham
10 Twiston

NEWCHURCH IN PENDLE
11 Goldshaw Booth
12 Barley with Wheatley Booth
13 Roughlee Booth
14 Old Laund Booth

COLNE
15 Colne
16 Barrowford
17 Foulridge
18 Trawden
19 Great and Little Marsden

PADIHAM
20 Padiham
21 Read
22 Simonstone
23 Hapton

BURNLEY
24 Burnley
25 Habergham Eaves
26 Briercliffe with Extwistle
27 Worsthorne with Hurstwood
28 Cliviger

ALTHAM
29 Altham
30 Clayton le Moors

CHURCH
31 Church
32 Oswaldtwistle
33 Huncoat

ACCRINGTON
34 Old Accrington
35 New Accrington

HASLINGDEN
36 Haslingden
37 Lower Booths
38 Higher Booths

NEWCHURCH IN ROSSENDALE
39 Newchurch

EXTRA-PAROCHIAL
40 Clitheroe Castle
41 Little Bowland
42 Leagram
43 Heyhouses
44 Higham with West Close Booth
45 Wheatley Carr Booth
46 Reedley Hallows, Filly Close, and New Laund Booth
47 Ightenhill Park
48 Dunnockshaw
49 Henheads

LANCASHIRE
Liverpool Manchester

8 Sunday 21 July 1822 in Camerton, Somerset

John Skinner (1772–1839), rector of Camerton from 1800, kept a voluminous record of his life. Often at odds with his unruly parishioners, who included coal miners and nonconformists, in 1822 he was having particular trouble with 'musical mutineers'. The bellringers were paid whenever they performed and invariably spent their takings on drink. The week before this diary entry, the drunken ringers had walked out of church when Skinner refused to let them chant the evening service as they usually did.

BL Add. MS 33673, ff.18v–19

without church or manor. Villages in, say, 1700 predominated over only about half the country, though they housed rather more than half the rural population. Over the rest of England, most people lived in hamlets or scattered farmhouses and cottages. As the rural population increased sharply in the late 18th and early 19th century, many smaller settlements were swollen to village size. Conversely, at the time of Domesday Book in 1086 and again after the Black Death in the mid 14th century, many settlements were so small as to be hardly recognisable as villages even when they possessed those 'essential' features of the village, a manor house and a parish church.

Many beginners in local history are unnecessarily confused by the complex relationship of parishes, manors, and villages, to say nothing of other overlapping or intermediate units such as townships, chapelries, hundreds, and rural deaneries. In fact, most local historians interested in a particular place do not have any difficulty at all: a hamlet, a village, or a group of small settlements served by one parish church normally bears a single name which expresses its unity and its identity as a community deserving separate study.

The basic unit of English topography is really not the parish but the township. Neither term is as widely understood as it should be. In the lowland counties of southern, eastern, and midland England most parishes contained only one township, though there were exceptions in all regions. Cambridgeshire is a good example (6). In the West Country and the North it was the single-township parish that was exceptional; most parishes had several townships and some contained very many. The huge parish of Whalley in north-east Lancashire included as many as 49 townships, some of them chapelries which functioned for some purposes as if they were parishes (7). Local historians in some counties will therefore think in terms of townships as the basic unit in the countryside, while others will think of parishes.

Parishes originated in England between the 10th and 12th centuries as the Church's provision of buildings and clergy at a local level was gradually reorganised. Boundaries between parishes were fixed when the payment of tithes (a tenth of the annual produce of the land for the support of the local clergy) was enforced, since it was necessary to know in which parish every piece of productive land owed tithes.

Until the 19th century, and in some areas into the 20th, townships and parishes were real communities, whose inhabitants were bound together in many different ways. Only the most obvious can be examined here. In the Middle Ages and later the parish was first of all a community of worshippers. When dissenting congregations were organised in the 1650s and later, that community began to break down, but even then the decline was slow and protracted. Only in the late 18th and 19th centuries, with the rise of rural Methodism and the general decline of religious observance, did it disappear from many parishes (8).

The history of a parish as a community of worshippers is expressed above all in the church itself (9). In the early modern period the local Christian community was also reflected in the foundation and upkeep of charities for the poor or for educational purposes. Many such charities had a continuous history until superseded by other forms of provision in the 19th century. Although it can sometimes be difficult to get behind the dry institutional shells of local charities, their records testify to one of the practical ways in which the inhabitants of a parish lived a common life (10).

The religious and charitable life of a community is not a self-contained topic isolated from economic activity or social relations. For instance, the fabric of a church building has a great deal to tell about other aspects of the community which used it; phases of extension and demolition and the richness of decoration and furnishings tell much about the size and wealth of the community at different periods. The parish church was also used as a focus for a great many non-religious activities. Meetings to decide village affairs were commonly held there, and in a later age the church door was the place where official notices were nailed.

The character of the parish was altered in the 16th century, as central government responded to social and economic change by delegating new tasks. Parishes or townships, according to region, took on new responsibilities, notably in the administration of the Elizabethan

9 Model of the parish church, Wroughton, Wiltshire
This model, made in 1839, shows many features which reflect the services held in Anglican churches in the 18th century. There is an elaborate pulpit but the chancel looks neglected. High-sided box pews gave warmth and privacy to churchgoers. Music would be provided by a church band in the upper gallery against the tower. The interior was redesigned in 1846 to provide a setting more suitable for the services favoured in the mid 19th century. The galleries and box pews were dismantled, and choir stalls and an organ were put in the chancel, which became the focus of services.
Photograph by A. P. Baggs

poor law through local overseers and in the maintenance of roads and bridges.

The secular role of parishes and townships made them even more important from the 16th century to the 19th as expressions of local communities. While remaining, for a time, communities of worshippers, early modern parishes were also communities which levied locally set rates to maintain their own paupers, repaired their own roads, kept the peace and handed serious offenders to higher judicial authorities, and did a host of other things. All these activities generated quantities of written records which are an invaluable source for anyone prepared to invest a little time in mastering the often difficult handwriting (11).

Manors

Other types of local community have overlapped with parishes at different periods. In the Middle Ages the manor was preeminent. The importance of manors to topography is great and the medieval period cannot be tackled without an understanding of what they were, but apart from Domesday Book, the records which cast light on them are almost all unpublished and written in heavily abbreviated Latin in a difficult script. Most of them are located in London.

Manors were a form of landed estate with certain distinct characteristics. Their main feature was that they had tenants over whom the lord of the manor exercised jurisdiction through a manorial court. The most characteristic type of tenants came to be known as 'copyholders' because their tenancies were authenticated by possession of

Mr. JOHN HODGSON, (a Quaker,) Steward to Lord Thanet.

[Those parts of the examination of this witness, which refer wholly to the property of the hospital, are not repeated here, the substance of them being fully stated in the Report.]

ARE you the steward of the Earl of Thanet?—I am, for his Yorkshire estates.

Do you, as the steward of the Earl of Thanet, receive the rents of the estates belonging to Beamsley hospital?—I do.

[Witness stated the total annual income of the hospital to be £.357. 9s. 4d.]

In what manner is the income applied?—It is applied in payment to the reader and almswomen, in an allowance to the minister of Bolton for administering the sacrament, in coals, and in such occasional repairs as I see necessary; and in payment of my own salary as agent.

What are the annual stipends of the reader and almswomen?—They are £.20 to the reader, £.18 to the matron, and £.16 each to 12 sisters.

How long have the stipends been of this amount?—Previous to Midsummer 1808, the stipends of the sisters were £.11 per annum; they were then increased to £.14; from March 1810, they were advanced to their present amount. The stipend of the reader was advanced in 1808 from £.18 to £.20. The stipend of the mother has been advanced from time to time with the others.

Have the almspeople any other allowance besides their stipends?—An allowance of coals, which has always been made, and which was increased last year.

What are the particulars of the other items of the expenditure?—To the clergyman, for administering the sacrament, £.1. 10s. a-year, and £.1 a-year for providing wine for the sacrament. My own salary, for mangement of the hospital accounts, £.10.; for coals in the last year, £.14; and for repairs upon an average, about £.3 or £.4 a-year. The total amount of the general expenditure as above stated, is £.260, or thereabouts.

10 Beamsley Hospital, Yorkshire, West Riding

The hospital, founded by Margaret Clifford, countess of Cumberland (25), never really broke free from the control of her descendants. In the 1810s the endowments were managed by the earl of Thanet's steward, and the sisters and mother were appointed by the earl on the recommendation of the leading inhabitants of Skipton and adjoining places. It played a limited part in relieving poverty in the area.
BL Official Publications Library, House of Commons Sessional Papers (1820), iv, *3rd Report of the Charity Commissioners*, appendix, p.251

a copy of the official record of the manorial court's proceedings (court rolls and, later, court books) in which changes of tenancy by inheritance or sale were sanctioned and recorded (12).

The medieval manor court carried out a wide variety of business besides registering changes in ownership of copyhold land. It enforced law and order and often maintained a complex system of by-laws to regulate agricultural practices within the manor. It is impossible to generalise about how closely the tenants of a manor, and in particular the persons named in a series of court rolls, corresponded with a local community. In most districts the fit between manors and communities was probably not exact, but it is frequently possible to be certain about which settlements a manor covered and how completely it covered them.

Communities at work

Small rural communities at all times until the 20th century have also invariably had in common their economic activities, by sharing in the farming of a particular area of land. The sense of belonging to an economic community must have been strongest in areas where the open-field system of agriculture prevailed. There, the ploughed land had not yet been cut up into privately owned 'fields' of the modern type (properly called 'closes') but lay in great unhedged tracts, each farmer possessing a number of narrow strips of land dispersed about the whole. Agriculture in such a system was regulated communally, though land was owned privately. Even in those parts of the country where open fields had more or less been swept away, or had never

11 Churchwarden's accounts from Wistaston, Cheshire

Churchwarden's accounts record money spent on holding services and maintaining the fabric of the church. This is part of Robert Perrin's accounts for Wistaston, near Nantwich in Cheshire, for 1780. It includes payments on 13 May 'for sacriment wine' for communion, on 28 May 'for makeing a new bell wheell & other repairs', and 10s. on 18 October 'spent at vissetation dinner & ale', refreshments on the day of the regular 'visitation' by officials from the diocese.

BL Add. MS 34818, f.238

12 Copyhold

This document is a 'copy of court roll', an official extract from the court roll of the earl of Oxford's manor of Laughton in Sussex given to one of the tenants. It is in Latin, and records that John Hokman the younger held a tenement and one yardland (in effect a small farm) in Shitynggclegh (a field name). It is dated Thursday, the morrow of the Circumcision in the 44th year of Edward III, in modern terms 2 January 1371.
BL Add. Charter 30352

existed in the first place, there was normally a need for communal management of common grazing land and hay meadows. Typically, the common grazing would be restricted to a set number of animals at different times in the year for each holder of a common right, while hay meadows were often staked out afresh each year and allotted among the commoners on a kind of rota.

The management of common land and open fields needed cooperation among peasant farmers, the acquiescence of lords of manors, and a system of electing accountable officials. At one extreme, the parishes on the fen edge north of Cambridge, which had open fields and extensive fen commons, boasted a highly complex arrangement of field reeves, fen reeves, haywards, pinders, and treasurers, some elected by the commoners and others appointed by the lords of manors. Where documents survive for such places they tell much about agricultural practices besides revealing how the community regulated its own affairs. Painstaking work can reveal, for instance, whether the elected offices were monopolised by the larger farmers or shared more equally.

The sense of studying a community located in a particular place is greatly enhanced if the fabric and layout of the settlement and the disposition of the fields, woods, and other features are taken as part of the same story. W. G. Hoskins was the first local historian to understand the intimacy of the connection between local community and local landscape and how far each can be understood only in the light of the other. His classic *The Making of the English Landscape* has now been superseded in many details by new interpretations of the age and development of landscape features, but the importance of studying landscapes and communities together is still great (13).

In pre-industrial England, the different types of communal bonds discussed in this chapter—religious, civil, and economic—reinforced one another to a remarkable degree. It is difficult now, even for those who live in agricultural villages, to imagine the intensity of social links in a community in which you saw all your neighbours in church, discussed with them the vital questions of farming, depended on some to carry out important tasks on behalf of all, and knew all their gossip. Only in the rare cases where one of the community turned chronicler, like Richard Gough at Myddle in Shropshire in 1701-2, is such an intensely face-to-face society depicted directly, but some of the records which relate to an individual place can begin to give an idea of it.

In the 19th century the old self-sufficient community of the English countryside was rapidly broken down at all levels by the intrusion of modern life. The final dissolution of the community of worshippers, the stripping away of local self-government from parishes and townships, and the inclosure movement which swept aside communally-regulated agriculture were only the most obvious assaults. The end of one old community in Hertfordshire, traced by B. J. Davey in *Ashwell 1830-1941: the Decline of a Village Community*, typifies some of the processes.

One factor alone remained of widespread importance, and that was one which had always been present, though perhaps not so obvious in comparison with the others: simply, residence in the same small place. Even when farmers could make decisions about their work independently of their neighbours, even when labourers were responsible solely to their employers, even when a free decision whether to attend church or chapel or not at all was possible, there remained the fact that people saw each other every day. The final bond of residence and identity with a particular place, evident in Flora Thompson's lightly fictionalised account of life in a north Oxfordshire hamlet, *Lark Rise to Candleford*, was broken only when widely available motor cars made possible long-distance day-to-day mobility.

13 **Willingham mere, Cambridgeshire**
Aerial photographs can reveal a great deal about past landscapes. This one has in the background the villages of Willingham and Over and in the foreground the site of a drained mere; the shells of freshwater molluscs have made the former bed show up white against the darker soils of the fens. There is much documentary evidence about how the mere and the fens provided a livelihood for the villagers in the Middle Ages and later, and about how the mere was eventually drained and the effects that its disappearance had on the two communities.
Cambridge University Collection of Air Photographs, BEZ-95

St. Albans : Clock Tower and Market Place

Towns and cities are not simply villages on a large scale. Apart from having more people, their economic and social structures are much more complex, and for the historian the amount of evidence to be assessed is likely to be vastly greater, even for a small market town, let alone a county town or a populous 19th-century industrial centre. There are simply too many sources for most part-time researchers to complete a study of a town on anything like as comprehensive a scale as could be attempted for a village. Some selectivity in topic or period or both is virtually essential.

The general story of a particular town should not, however, be ignored. It is especially important to have an acquaintance with the overall shape of the town's past when you are working on only a short period in the history of a long-established town or on a single suburb of a great city. Fortunately, for towns even more than for villages, the means are usually to hand. Nineteenth-century civic pride ensured that virtually all towns have at least one published history, however antiquarian in tone and however inadequate it may seem today. Even outdated town histories should be read through with some care. If for no other reason, they will give some indication as to which parts of a town's past are most interesting, best documented, or have been neglected. They are particularly likely to cover in some detail the constitutional history of an older town, the staple fare of

19th-century urban history which may now seem old-fashioned, but is nevertheless essential. Conversely, older town histories will normally have ignored such matters as physical growth and social structure, which are quite manageable topics for research.

Most local historians would be daunted by the prospect of tackling the whole of one of the larger provincial cities, let alone London, even over a short period. It is also reasonable to assume that a town or city much above a population of 100,000 may not have so strong a pull on the affections and interests of local historians as particular parts of it. Even a smaller town with a long history will take an inordinate amount of time. There is, however, an important place for the reinterpretation of the whole history of a town, though it needs experience of research and a wide knowledge of English history to be contemplated. John Chandler's book on Salisbury, *Endless Street*, is a good example of a justifiable new look at a historically well-known town. By concentrating on the essentials and shifting the focus away from the institutional obsessions of the 19th century towards economic and social matters and the fabric of the town it will often be possible to retell a familiar tale in a completely new way.

Chandler's Salisbury sets a useful agenda for the topics with which the historian of a town should become familiar, however restricted the subject actually being researched. He begins with population, the main index and often the agent of the changing fortunes of a town. Information on population levels before the 19th century does not come in the form of a count of individuals which can be directly compared with the figures in the 1801 and later censuses. It is normally possible to estimate a range of population from lists of taxpayers (**14**), households, or communicants, making due allowance for the probable extent of evasion, size of households, and proportion of children in the total. It is more convincing and useful historically not to pay too much attention to the absolute size of a town's population but to compare it with other towns in the vicinity (or the country at large) in order to get some idea of its ranking.

Chandler takes as his second theme the economic history of Salisbury, paying particular attention to two of its leading characteristics, the rise and fall of the medieval cloth-making industry and the town's enduring importance as a marketing centre for a wide region. Clearly there will be many different approaches to the economy of towns, since their characteristics differed greatly. The idea of Salisbury as a regional centre is further explored in a chapter on communications. A chapter on local government was deliberately kept short because the author felt that the subject had been fully explored in earlier studies of the town and that it was necessary only to summarise. Finally, Chandler examines the ordinary lives of the people of Salisbury through the ages, for instance by sampling early-modern probate inventories, conducting a guided tour of a small area of the town in the 1871 census, and using a good collection of property deeds

OPPOSITE

14 Tax assessment, Colchester
The assessment was for a tax granted
by parliament to Henry VII in
1489; the full list of names for Colchester survives. In St Leonard's
parish, the town's port called the
Hythe (1, 5), 50 householders were
taxed. Given that there would be
others too poor to be assessed, the
population must have been of the
order of 400. The population of Colchester as a whole in 1524 has been
estimated as about 5,300, perhaps a
considerable increase over 1489 since
the number of taxpayers had grown
by two fifths.
BL Stowe MS 828, f.21v

to tell the story of a single surviving medieval house. The physical
growth of Salisbury, which is mentioned in several of the chapters,
might have been treated as a distinct theme.

Urban history since the Industrial Revolution

The beginner is not likely to rush into writing the history of a town
on such an ambitious scale and the rest of this chapter is written in
the expectation that the reader has in mind a particular topic or period
in addition to a particular place.

Some of the best local history manuals advise those interested in
towns to confine themselves to the 19th century, or at least to begin
there. The advice is soundly based on the existence of such staple evidence as census returns, large-scale Ordnance Survey maps, and
surviving buildings and other features of the urban landscape. The
focusing of interest on the 19th century also makes sense in the light
of the growing urbanisation of the country in that period. Already by
1851 half the population of England lived in urban areas and nearly
a quarter in the ten biggest cities with more than 100,000 inhabitants
each. By 1911 four-fifths of the population was urban and almost half
was concentrated in cities over 100,000. Local historians who research
late 19th-century towns are dealing with the most common experience
of ordinary people at that time.

The physical spread of all towns and cities in the late 19th century
and even more in the 20th means that local historians are often concerned with places that were outlying villages until swamped by a
growing town in recent times. The approaches of rural and urban
history will therefore often be combined and it would certainly be a
mistake to try to write about, say, Islington, without having London
in mind (15).

Much has been written, both by local historians and by national
historians using local evidence, about the growth of towns, the formation of suburbs, and the suburbanisation of villages. Given that
suburbanisation was taking place at a time when mass communications and mass building methods were in use, and when the country
was becoming increasingly homogenised, it is not surprising that
certain features of the development of suburbs recur time and again
in different parts of the country. Rural places continued to differ
much more sharply from one another throughout the 19th century
than did urban places. The historian of a suburb can therefore learn
a great deal from reading about other suburbs. It is common to find,
for instance, that a growing town lost from its central area first the
upper middle classes, who built large houses in spacious grounds, and
then the rest of the working population. The houses of the first sub-
urban pioneers were often demolished but the terraced and semi-
detached houses which displaced them had to be fitted into an existing
pattern of separately owned estates. Such a pattern has been found,

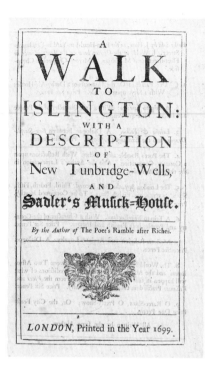

15 A country walk in London, 1699
The area round the present Sadler's Wells theatre half a mile north of the City of London, though not built over until the early 19th century, was much frequented by Londoners from 1683, when supposedly medicinal springs were discovered. In the late 17th century Thomas Sadler provided refreshments and diversions at a 'Musick-House' nearby. These satirical verses by Edward Ward, published in 1699, described the dubious entertainments on offer. BL Printed Books, Tab.4.b.4, no.4

for instance, by H. J. Dyos in Camberwell and by Maurice Beresford in the small area of Leeds which was further transformed in the 1960s into the university campus. Despite common traits, every suburb and every town will be sufficiently different to make a detailed investigation of its 19th-century history well worth while.

Pre-industrial urban history

No two towns are alike, but for the present purpose only two categories of urban history need to be distinguished: the sort that deals with late 18th-, 19th-, and 20th-century towns in the throes of the Industrial Revolution and 'pre-industrial' urban history. The latter is perhaps a misnomer, since 'pre-industrial' towns certainly did not lack industries. A division of urban history into two types does not imply two exclusive sorts of towns, old and new. A few old towns have failed to retain urban status to the present day. Dunwich in Suffolk, a great medieval town whose gravelly site was progressively washed away by the North Sea, is an example. Conversely, a handful of new 19th-century towns, like Scunthorpe and Southsea, grew up by design or accident in the middle of purely rural areas or as coastal resorts. Most towns, however, have always had some urban characteristics. It is therefore quite feasible to study an ancient non-industrialised town in the 19th century, or the great industrial cities of the North in the Middle Ages. On the whole, however, it is fair to assume that local historians in, say, Marlborough are more likely to have their imagination fired by some more distant part of its story, while Mancunians and Liverpudlians will rightly feel that the 18th and 19th centuries were a more important era for their towns than the Middle Ages.

Pre-industrial towns varied greatly in character and complexity, but even for quite small ones there will be an abundance of evidence for almost all periods. A village with good medieval accounts or court rolls cannot begin to compare with a small town in the sheer unwieldly bulk of documentary evidence that will be available. One characteristic complication in towns is the existence of craft guilds, whose records (PLATE 2) reflect the institutional apparatus, economic structure, and social life of a town. Good Latin, practice in reading old handwriting, and a great deal of time, patience, and organisation are required to make sense of such documents, and it would be wrong to advise beginners to plunge straight into medieval or early modern urban history. Even with the older English towns, it is better to begin in the 19th century and work backwards.

Beginning urban history

The amount of evidence surviving for 19th-century towns will of course be even bulkier, often intractably so, but at least it is easier

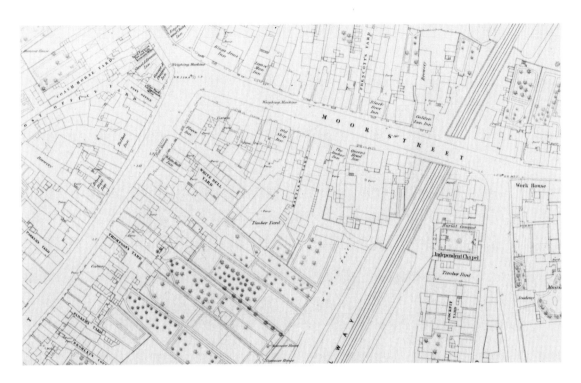

16 Ormskirk, Lancashire, in 1848
Ormskirk was surveyed for the Ordnance Survey series of town plans in
1848-9 and published at the scale of
5 feet to 1 mile (1/1,056) in 1851.
The detail extends to the location of
communal wells and pumps in the
poorer parts of town. The map illustrates very clearly how crowded and
insanitary courts existed alongside
middle-class houses with spacious
gardens. In the late 1840s the courts
were packed with destitute and
disease-ridden Irish emigrants.
BL Maps, OST 83, sheet 3

to read and more likely to be found locally than in the national
libraries and record offices in London. More or less all towns have
a range of standard sources for the 19th century: large-scale Ordnance
Survey maps; detailed street directories; surviving buildings which
may not survive for much longer (for example, mid 19th-century
working-class housing); newspapers (often unindexed); and
'ephemera', a category which covers everything from sale particulars
to notices of church bazaars and will often have been gathered
together in a local studies library. The normal approach for a beginner
might be to take one or more of them as a basis for getting a good
picture of a town at a particular moment in time, then work outwards
to other sources for a topic which seems worth further study. There
is no better place to start than the splendid series of Ordnance Survey
town plans (16), whose marvellous detail of streets, houses, factories,
and public buildings can hardly fail to make the beginner want to
know more.

Most towns have so much information available about their recent
past that some local historians are tempted simply to pile it up, fact
on fact, in a great heap of undifferentiated knowledge about the past.
Though valuable as a chronicle of the past, at least if indexed, accessible, and supported by references to the original sources of the information, it should not be mistaken for local history itself.

A better starting point for an approach to the history of a town or
suburb is not the collection of facts but a single vital question: what

**17 Hosiery workshops, Tewkes-
bury, Gloucestershire**
The two cottages on the right and a
third out of view were built about
1780 for use by stocking knitters.
Each originally had one room on
each floor, linked by a narrow spiral
staircase. The first-floor rooms
housed the knitting frames and the
other floors were for domestic use. In
1810 there were three stocking knitters in St Mary's Lane and 800
frames in the town. The Landmark
Trust acquired two of the derelict
cottages in 1970 and the third in
1982 and has since restored them.
National Monuments Record, BB
70/395

distinguishes this town from others? It is likely to be something which
everybody who knows the town knows already. Does it have a characteristic industry? Is it a market centre, an engineering town, a textile
town? If textiles, was it wool, cotton, silk, or linen? If cotton, was
it spinning or weaving?

Characteristic trades or industries have been a feature of long-
established towns as well as the 19th-century boom towns of the
industrial North and Midlands. Tewkesbury, for instance, though a
market town and riverside entrepôt involved in a wide variety of trad-
ing activity in pre-industrial times (PLATE 6), also had its specialisations. It was once renowned for mustard (there is a reference in
Shakespeare's *Henry IV, Part 2*), though virtually no evidence can
be found for how the manufacture or sale of mustard was organised
in Tewkesbury. A better documented trade is framework knitting of
stockings, important from the late 17th century until competition
from factory production in other districts in the mid 19th century
destroyed it. The importance of framework knitting in Tewkesbury
can be gauged in outline from visitors' descriptions of the town. Evidence about the carriage of knitted stockings down the Severn can
be gathered from the Gloucester port books. Parliamentary investiga-
tions into the industry in the 19th century provide statistics and often
go into fine detail about particular enterprises, though not for Tewkesbury. There are contemporary illustrations, directories, and census
enumerators' books. Documentary references to the location of
hosiery workshops in the town can be matched with the evidence of
surviving buildings and demolished ones known from old photographs. Nos 28-32 St Mary's Lane, for instance, have the wide upper-
storey windows needed to give enough light for framework knitting
(17).

A different set of questions can be asked about the appearance of
a town or suburb. Were the 19th-century terraced houses (whether
surviving or demolished) different from those in nearby places? Were
they brick or stone, and were there local brickworks or quarries? Were
they largely back-to-backs, arranged as flats on separate floors, terraced with wide back streets, or in some other arrangement? Do they
mainly date from before or after those in neighbouring towns or
adjoining suburbs?

The questions which it is possible to ask at the outset of research
on a town from simple observation could be multiplied almost indefi-
nitely. What is most needed when the task of finding answers begins
is a sense of where your own particular front of research contributes
to an understanding of the history of the town as a whole.

VIEW OF DANBY

Local historians know that all places are different. They should also understand that some are less different than others. The existence of common themes in the history of neighbouring places is one of the two points from which local history can and must extend itself into regional history. One of the things that regional historians do is to make patterns of the similarities and dissimilarities and also of the inevitable links between neighbouring places in order to define regions. The second point of departure into regional history has to do with local history's concern with individuals in particular places in the past and can best be grasped by thinking how an imaginary Yorkshirewoman might describe where she was from if asked by a stranger. It would vary according to circumstance. If asked in Paris she might say 'England'; if in London, 'Yorkshire'; if in Leeds, 'Pontefract'; if in Pontefract, she might have to specify the street where she lived to give a satisfactory answer. Furthermore, she might regard herself as being 'from' each of those places even if it was 50 years since she had lived there. All individuals inhabit the centre spot in a nest of concentric circles which include not only a variety of geographical locations of varying precision but also different social circumstances of family, work, and class. Both points of departure for local historians lead both to regional history and also to national history, which is reserved for the following chapter.

Types of regional history

Historians study regions for different reasons and they study different types of region. Before suggesting how regional history is appropriate for local historians it might be helpful to indicate the main types. On a geographical scale, what passes for a region can be as small as a few adjacent parishes sharing a particular type of landscape, or as large as one of the major subdivisions of the country like East Anglia or the North. In the middle of the range comes the county, which has always exerted a particular attraction on local historians, for reasons of sentiment as much as the practical advantages connected with the accessibility of documents.

The historical regions of England are elusive. Their boundaries

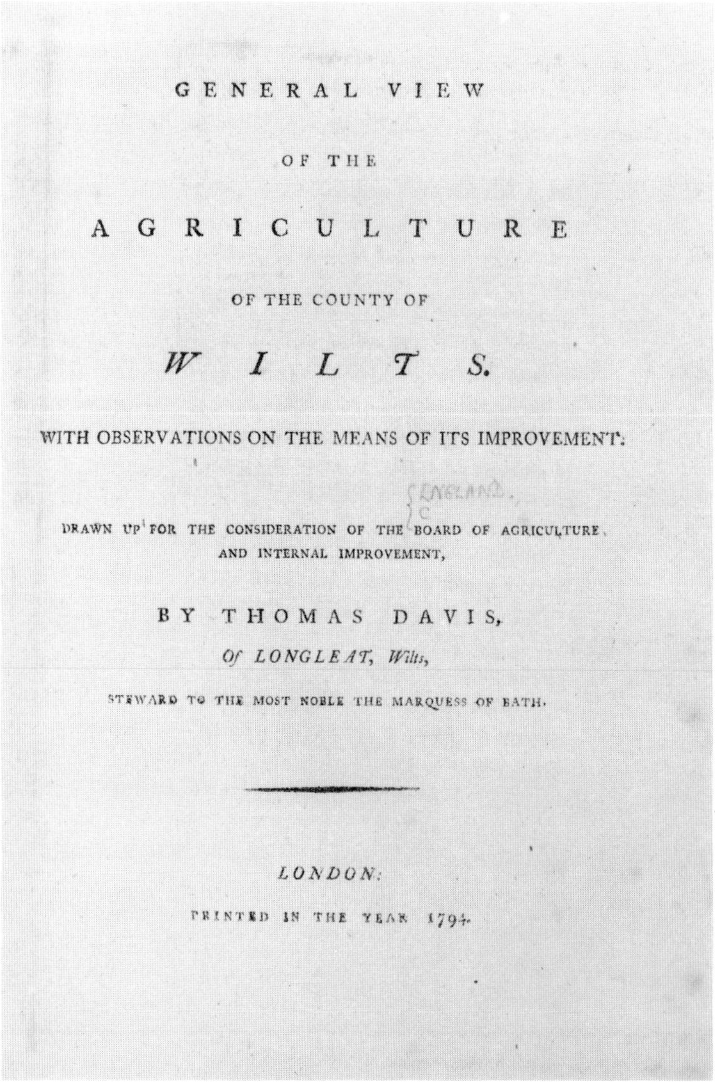

18 Wiltshire agriculture in the 1790s
The Board of Agriculture, set up in 1793, sponsored two series of county reports on agriculture. The first, published between 1793 and 1796, was intended to be circulated to farmers and landowners for their comments; all counties had a second report published later. They are invaluable sources for agricultural history, even though some of the writers stressed improved farming methods within their county at the expense of what was more typical. Davis's *Wiltshire* has been called 'perhaps the best of all the agricultural reports'.
BL Printed Books, Ac.3484/6 (3)

GENERAL VIEW

OF THE

AGRICULTURE

OF THE COUNTY OF

W I L T S.

WITH OBSERVATIONS ON THE MEANS OF ITS IMPROVEMENT:

DRAWN UP FOR THE CONSIDERATION OF THE BOARD OF AGRICULTURE, AND INTERNAL IMPROVEMENT,

BY THOMAS DAVIS,

Of LONGLEAT, Wilts,

STEWARD TO THE MOST NOBLE THE MARQUESS OF BATH.

LONDON:

PRINTED IN THE YEAR 1794.

19 Wiltshire farming regions
Wiltshire was described as a county
of chalk and cheese by John Aubrey
in the 1680s. In the 1790s Thomas
Davis (**18**) drew a map similar to this
one, but it was only the researches of
Eric Kerridge in the 20th century
which showed the detailed differences between regions. For instance, although the Chalk, Corallian, and Cotswold countries all
followed sheep and corn husbandry
in the 16th, 17th, and 18th centuries,
there were variations; the Cotswolds
also had some dairying, while the
Corallian limestone ridge was largely
inclosed, in contrast to the open
arable fields and sheep downs of the
Chalk.
Map redrawn from *VCH Wiltshire*,
iv, p.43

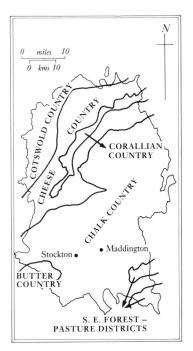

were not static over time and within a single period the same
boundaries cannot necessarily be used when examining phenomena
as varied as economic links and political communities. Researchers
looking at, for example, the economic relations of an individual town
and its rural hinterland will find it necessary to widen or foreshorten
their perspective for different periods of the past. To revert to an
example used in the last chapter, the territory from which Tewkesbury drew raw materials and labour presumably expanded and con-
tracted with the rise and decline of the hosiery trade.

Some of the more important types of region which local historians
are likely to find being written about are political regions, farming
regions, so-called *pays*, urban hinterlands, and 'neighbourhoods'. It
is not proposed to discuss purely administrative districts or to pay
more than passing attention to the 'county communities' which are
often encountered in studies of political activity.

Farming regions have the longest pedigree of all in regional studies,
though their importance has perhaps only been fully brought out in
the last 40 years. Joan Thirsk, in the collaborative *Agrarian History
of England and Wales* for the period 1500-1640, and others have
shown how the country can be divided into a series of regions according to the nature of the farming which was carried on within them.
Earlier writers on agriculture, who had normally described whole
counties (**18**), had of course recognised that the agricultural conditions
and practices of individual counties were not usually uniform, but the
variations were not mapped so subtly until the 1960s. For instance,
Wiltshire had long been acknowledged as a county of chalk and
cheese, partly comprising chalk downland grazed by enormous flocks
of sheep and partly fertile river valleys used for dairy herds. More
systematic investigation has made it possible to draw a more detailed
and sophisticated map of the farming districts of the county (**19**).

The significance of the 'discovery' of farming regions was not
limited to agriculture alone. The type of farming suited to a particular
region affected the size of farms and so the social status of farmers,
the number and skills of farm hands required and whether they were
best accommodated in the farmers' households or in their own cottages, besides a host of other arrangements which carry over into
social rather than purely economic history (**20**).

Farming regions overlap as a type of region with what have been
termed, borrowing a French word, *pays*, but might be given the more
homely name of 'countrysides'. The idea is that natural geographical
features such as ranges of hills, river valleys, or extensive tracts of fen
or woodland imposed certain constraints in the pre-industrial period,
notably on the type of agriculture that could be practised. A typical
countryside is a small area over which geographical conditions are
relatively uniform. Thus in Kent, Alan Everitt has recently identified
six distinct regions, which he calls, adopting some old names and
inventing some new ones, Foothills, Downland, Holmesdale,

20 A Wiltshire farm in 1881

The numerous 19th-century Royal Commissions on agriculture often give valuable details about individual farms straight from the mouths of farmers who were called as witnesses. Edwin Lywood, here giving evidence on 29 June 1881, had rented a large farm at Maddington in the Chalk region (19) since 1866 and was able to give precise details of his labour costs and prices to the Commission, besides this information about his work force. He had 15 tied cottages for his men.
BL Official Publications Library, House of Commons Sessional Papers (1881), xvii, *Minutes of Evidence taken before Commission on Agriculture* [C.3096]

50,648. With regard to this labour question, how many men do you employ on the average; how many shepherds do you keep?—I keep five shepherds for 1,000 ewes, and about 300 young sheep.

50,649. How many horsemen have you?—Fourteen men and boys.

50,650. And how many ordinary labourers?—They vary in winter and summer.

50,651. I take the average. Of course you do not pay them on wet days?—Yes, all the regular men are paid on wet days.

50,652. You pay so much per week, wet and dry?—Yes.

50,653. Then how many hands upon the whole do you employ upon an average, men and boys?—Altogether, I fancy, about 30 in the winter.

50,654. And how many in the summer?—They vary in the summer.

50,655. How many of those shepherds are boys, or what we call pages in our country?—Three are men and two are lads, with two other men in the winter in the lambing time.

50,656. Have you five men and two boys to 1,000 ewes and 300 dry sheep?—Yes, during the lambing season.

50,657. I suppose that they do all the carting and topping, and cutting turnips, and everything else?—No, I have extra men carting besides.

50,658. Had you a strike in your district?—Some years ago.

50,659. Seven years ago?—I think more than that; I think it was 10 years ago.

50,660. Do the men work well now?—Yes, our men work fairly well.

Chartland, Weald, and Marshland. In general, though, the work of identifying the separate countrysides of England has not gone so far as the description of farming regions, partly because the boundaries between them can be extremely difficult to draw, leading to a multiplication of intermediate and transitional types.

Farming regions and *pays* are defined by assessing similarities and dissimilarities in physical characteristics of various kinds. Other ways of dividing England into regions have concentrated instead on searching for direct economic or social links between places. Notably, urban historians have tried to determine the extent of the hinterland of particular towns at different periods. Clearly, towns of different size and status affected the surrounding countryside in quite varying degrees.

A small market town in the 13th century, when markets were being established everywhere, would have had only a restricted catchment area, whereas at the other extreme, a research project into how medieval London was fed is ranging over as many as ten counties. At any one time an individual rural village would therefore feel the pull of a number of urban centres of different rank. Change over time has also to be taken into account.

A further type of area, with the provisional name of 'neighbourhood', has recently been added to the array of regions. Although it was rare for a family to stay settled in one place for more than a few generations, most movements for marriage or work were over short distances. It has thus been found, for instance, that many surnames congregated within a limited district rather than spreading widely. Cultural links expressed through local customs and dialect were reinforced by the limited range of most people's movements. How such links built up to form regional patterns has not yet been discovered by historians. It is possible that each village stood at the centre of its own web of connections made by marriage and migration and that no web was tighter than any other, or alternatively that genuine 'neighbourhoods' of groups of villages bound by specially dense networks of links can be discovered by patient work.

Places and regions

The varieties of regional history on offer mean that part-time local historians can approach regions in a number of ways. Perhaps the most common for the great majority of local historians interested first and foremost in a particular place is to regard the wider region as a means of understanding their chosen place better. You will in fact probably have to keep in mind both a ring of concentric regions and a cluster of overlapping regions, each appropriate in a different way. Historians of Burnley in Lancashire will thus take as their region for the 19th century that part of east Lancashire which was busy spinning and weaving cotton for sale through Manchester. For the early modern period, when the cloth made locally was woollen and the centre of the trade lay at Halifax in Yorkshire, the natural region is a trans-Pennine one which does not extend to Manchester. Going back still further, to the late Middle Ages, Burnley will be examined as one component in the landed estate covering the whole of northeast Lancashire which went under the name of the honor of Clitheroe, while in the early Middle Ages, for which there is virtually no evidence specific to the district, sense can be made of the fragments only by looking at the broadly similar society and economy of northern England as a whole. Regions have to be chosen to fit both the circumstances and the evidence.

A second way of looking at regions is as the natural units for researching certain topics at less than national but more than local level. Some topics which form an integral part of the story of any individual place are not well suited, or not suited at all, to a parish-by-parish approach. Two subjects in particular are commonly quoted as falling into that category: agriculture and the landscape. Although it is possible in the end to write sensibly about the agriculture or the landscape of all but the smallest rural settlement, it is difficult to reach the necessary level of understanding by looking at only one place.

Especially for agricultural history, the two approaches to regions are complementary, since the evidence for any one place may well be too insubstantial (PLATE 4). It is not practicable to write a sustained historical account of the economy of a medieval parish if no court rolls or accounts and surveys survive, or of the economy of an 18th-century parish dominated by a single estate if its papers are lost or inaccessible. Such deficiencies clearly matter not at all to the national historian, who can pick any local examples which have good sources. They matter very much if the undocumented place is the only one you are interested in. For topographers looking at a particular place over a long period of time there are bound to be some subjects which could perfectly well be studied for some other village or town but for which there is no evidence at all for their own. In such circumstances one recourse is to explore the surrounding region for better documented places which will, by analogy, throw some light on the particular place under consideration. Another is to choose a group of adjoining places.

Counties

Few counties are sensible 'regions' for purposes other than the study of local government, despite their longevity from the 10th century, or earlier, until the present day (or 1974 for the unlucky ones). Even in social history the idea of a 'county community' is valid, if at all, only for a very limited echelon at the top of society and for a limited period. If anything to do with the economy or the land is under review, only a very few counties at the extremities of England, where geographical homogeneity is much stronger, make suitable regions, as in A.L.Rowse's classic *Tudor Cornwall*, which examines a peculiarly introverted regional society. A convincing region like Cumbria, whose landscape and society in the Middle Ages are the subject of a recent book by Angus Winchester, has been a county only since 1974, having previously been two and a bit. Other administratively defined districts may be equally misleading for regional history (21).

Yet many books by and for local historians have taken the county as their unalterable basis. The Victoria County History is only the most obvious example. The *English Landscape* series inspired by W.G.Hoskins used counties despite the fact that the regional landscapes of England are anything but neatly confined within county

OPPOSITE
21 List of places in Delamere forest
A medieval forest was a legal entity, which lay outside (Latin *foris*) the common law of England and under its own system of forest law, protecting the king's (or in Cheshire the earl's) hunting rights. This undated list of 62 'vills within the forest of Mara and Mondrem', the medieval name of Delamere, is therefore an administrative document. The landscape and the economic condition of the forest were not uniform. Besides some wooded areas and open heathland, ideal for hunting, there was a great deal of cultivated land in private hands.
BL Harley MS 2115, f.67v

boundaries. Archaeological and local history societies too, for reasons both historical and practical, respect county boundaries, while many self-styled regional divisions of the country turn out to be no more than groupings of counties.

There are two very good reasons for the practical way in which local history approaches the county and they both have to do with the longevity of the English counties. In the first place, the length of their survival has produced continuous series of historical records which either emanated from the counties or, in the case of the public records, were subdivided by counties. The existence of county societies for local history and of county record offices have in their different ways further encouraged county-based history. The classes in the Public Record Office are commonly arranged or indexed by county. For many of them it is easy to search through a class looking for all the references to places within a particular county, and inconvenient to do it for two. Secondly, county loyalties have become embedded in the psyche of the English race to an extraordinary degree and probably nowhere more so than in that small segment interested in their local past. We are first English and second devoted to a particular county. Even in the late 19th and early 20th century, when population growth, industrialisation, and migration were most likely to undermine county loyalties, the trend was counterbalanced by such factors as the rise of county sports teams and the attachment of army regiments to particular counties. There can hardly be a local historian in the land who is not fundamentally more interested in just one county rather than all the others. The pull of loyalty is the best justification of all for county history.

Archetypes and comparisons

Some of the most successful excursions into regional history have actually been case studies of particular localities framed with the idea of a wider region in mind. Thus W. G. Hoskins's *The Midland Peasant*, based on the single Leicestershire village of Wigston Magna, uses that one place as the archetype of the villages of the Midland clay lands. Even though Hoskins deliberately refrained from testing the typicality of Wigston, his study is required reading for anyone tracing the history of a community within a broadly similar setting. Other studies which have broadened out from the base of a small number of places to consider a region have been more explicitly comparative. Two of the best known concern Cambridgeshire villages. J. R. Ravensdale's *Liable to Floods* looked at three adjacent villages on the edge of the fens, Cottenham, Landbeach, and Waterbeach. By choosing three well-documented places with a similar landscape and economy he was able to explore how small variations in the terrain, such as the exact proportion and disposition of the slightly higher land suitable for arable farming, together with other factors such as land ownership, could create substantial differences in the economic system, social structure, and landscape history of the three parishes. The book is thus useful for anyone working on a place in low-lying fen country, not only the Cambridgeshire fens. Margaret Spufford's *Contrasting Communities* instead chose three Cambridgeshire villages from quite different 'countrysides': Orwell in the western clay 'uplands' of the county, Chippenham on the eastern chalk hills, and Willingham, a fen-edge village adjacent to Ravensdale's examples. By adopting a more limited time span than Ravensdale's (essentially the late 16th and the 17th century) she was able to show how the different economic possibilities inherent in the terrain of her three parishes affected other aspects of life there including land ownership and religious views.

Regional history is not the same thing as local history as it is usually understood. Intrinsically it is neither a 'better' nor a 'worse' version of history at a level below that of England as a whole. For some topics, one of the several varieties of regional history may be a more appropriate means of approach because of the nature of the sources or the character of the topic. Just as regional historians ignore at their peril the separate identity of individual places within the region, so historians of particular places need to keep in mind the different levels of regional society and economy to which their places belonged.

5 National History and Local History

THE STAFFORDSHIRE AND WORCESTERSHIRE CANAL,
KIDDERMINSTER

Local history and national history are parts of one subject, not opposites. Despite differences in their characteristic sources, methods, and outlook, and despite the fact that local historians are largely amateurs and national historians almost all professionals, they are both ultimately directed at a single objective. If history is simply defined as the study of man in the past, then the difference is at heart only that national historians are concerned with the set of people who lived inside a national boundary while local historians confine themselves to one or more smaller localities within the nation. Neither can

**22 The serfs of Cuxham,
Oxfordshire, in 1279**
The 'Hundred Rolls' of 1279 were
printed in a special typeface in the
1810s. Here, the rents and services
which John Hest owed to Merton
College, Oxford, as lord of Cuxham,
for his half yardland are said to
include working on the college's land
every other day except Sundays,
feast days, Christmas, Easter, and
Whitsun, and helping at harvest with
five other men. The second
paragraph lists the other serfs who
had similar obligations: Richard the
white, Gilbert Alan, Cecily the
widow, Gilbert son of Gilbert, Eve
the widow, Robert son of Richard,
and Isabel the widow.
BL Printed Books, G.10313, p.758

SERVI.

Joħes Heſt tenet dimiđ virgat' ħre villan' de þđco cuſtođ &
ſcolar' ſolvenđ p ann' j qᵃrꞇiū fꝶi & qᵃrtam pꞇē uniᵖ buſſeꞇ
fruɱti & dimiđ qᵃrꞇiū aven' Iꞇ iij gallin' & ij gallinas & j
gallū ij panes albas vꞇ vj d. p voluntate đni & unū obulū arꞡnti
& debet opari ſecundo die p totū ann' except' die Saꞗbi diebȝ
feſtivalibȝ feſto Nataꞇ Dñi feſto Paſcħ & Pent' iſtud svic' pot'
mutari p volūtate đni in qᶦnꝗ foliđ   Iꞇ debet filios & filias
rediɱe et debet opari in autūpno cū qᶦnꝗ hōibȝ.

Iꞇ Riꞔus le Wyte Gileꞗs Alein Cecilia Vidua Gileꞗs fiꞇ
Gileꞗi Eva Vidua Roꞗs fiꞇ Riꞔi Iſabeꞇ Vidua quilibȝ eoꝛ tenet
dimiđ virgat' ħre p eaſđē ꝯſuetuđ & eađē svic' in oɱibȝ qᶦ
facit þđcus Joħes.

afford to ignore the perspective of the other since they are alternative
points of view of the same people.

Individual men and women in the past belonged to individual
localities, to England at large, and to other geographically and socially
defined areas intermediate between place and nation and indeed to
areas which transcended nations or were contained within individual
settlements. Their history can be told in terms of any one of the
appropriate areas or a combination of them. Thus, the economic
fortunes of medieval English peasants can be investigated by researching one village intensively, as Paul Harvey did in *A Medieval Oxfordshire Village: Cuxham 1240-1400*, or by combining less detailed
evidence from several places, as writers of textbooks about the medieval economy have to do. The two approaches cannot be separated.
Harvey took full account of what was known at the time about the
medieval economy, but his study added so much more detailed information about precise conditions in a particular place that all subsequent discussions of the peasantry have had to take account of
Cuxham (**22**). Local history and national history are interdependent.
Earlier chapters in this book have stressed that local historians must
be aware of what was happening outside their chosen locality. It is
no less true that over an enormous range of topics, excluding only
the esoteric reaches of high finance and high politics, national history
cannot be written without a local dimension.

Generalising from the particular

It follows that the country as a whole is not a 'better' level than individual localities as a means of describing or explaining the past, except
for obvious aspects like foreign policy or the institutions of central
government. English history is simply a different level of generalisation from local history. Although W. G. Hoskins is of William Blake's

23 Fenland speed skating

Speed skating for prizes began in the Fens in the early 19th century. The contests between 1854 and 1867 were dominated by these two men, here shown in their 60s in 1895: William 'Turkey' Smart (right) and his nearest rival William 'Gutta-Percha' See, nicknamed respectively from a distinctive skating style and formidable toughness. Both were from Welney. There was intense competition among villages. The sport was put on a more regular basis with the formation in 1879 of the National Skating Association, which held regular timed championships over measured courses. Fen skating gradually lost its distinctive local flavour as it was merged into a national and international sport. Cambridgeshire Collection, Cambridge City Library, negative no.81/30/9

*Quoted in *Provincial England: Essays in Social and Economic History* (London, 1963) page v.

opinion that 'To Generalize is to be an Idiot. To Particularize is the Alone Distinction of Merit',* he has undermined it with every word that he has written. Indeed his strengths as a local historian, which should be a model for all, are precisely the ability to sum up the general development of a particular place without getting bogged down in the mire of detail, and then go on to show how the lessons of one place could be applied to others and to English history generally. Blake's epigram is a marvellous rallying cry for local history, but it would not do to take it seriously as a way of thinking about the past. The stories of towns and villages cannot be told without generalising. History without generalisation is antiquarianism, the collection of facts about the past without any thought about their relative significance. Moreover, while the economic and social history of the country at large often takes the form of single big generalisations based on a knowledge of individual case studies, local historians are required to generalise on several levels at once, not only about their own particular places but also keeping in mind how typical they were of wider regions around, including England generally.

National and local historians share much common ground. None of the four main branches of historical studies – political, economic, social, and cultural – stands fully apart from local factors, though in political history there is a natural division between the study of national politics and of local political activity. They are much more separate from one another than, say, national and local economic history. A general political history of England could be written convincingly without referring to a single place, but the same is not true of economic or social history. Conversely, a well-researched and well-written account of local politics, such as the political structure of a 19th-century town, might have no bearing on national politics, while a new study of its economy could not be ignored by national economic historians. Cultural history as the history of, say, fine art and its collectors often has a great deal to say about the history of certain social groups in London and the bigger provincial towns, while cultural history as the history of the way ordinary people thought is central to the interests of local historians. Social history is even more local in its associations (23).

The economic and social history of England is a vast area in which it is hardly possible to separate national and local approaches. Many admired recent syntheses, such as C. G. A. Clay's *Economic Expansion and Social Change: England 1500-1700*, are full of well-chosen examples of what was happening in particular regions, towns, and villages. New studies by local historians will continue to enrich textbook history by reminding its writers about the diversity of individual places and about the regional patterns which were superimposed upon the local variations.

The perspectives from which historians observe separate localities nevertheless differ fundamentally between national and local history. National historians see local studies as a contribution to writing about England as a whole. Whether they themselves sample well-documented places or rely on the work of others, they are essentially subordinating local experiences to their wish to generalise more widely. Conversely, local historians use available general accounts to provide a context for their own studies, subordinating the inevitably vaguer generalisations of national history to the more immediate reality of what happened in a particular place. The statements that the inclosure movement transformed half England between 1760 and 1840 and that the Nottinghamshire village of Widmerpool was transformed by parliamentary inclosure in 1804 represent different orders of historical explanation (24). They may both be true, though the latter is less likely to be modified by subsequent research or reinterpretation,

24 Widmerpool Inclosure Act
The inclosure act for Widmerpool, Nottinghamshire, was promoted by the main landowner in the parish, Charles Pierrepont, Viscount Newark. It was passed in 1802, the open fields being divided under an award of 1804. Almost 1,800 acres of the 2,100 acres of the parish were involved, transforming the landscape. In the 18th century there had been numerous small tenant farms, but the population fell sharply in the 1820s and 1840s.
BL Official Publications Library, Private Acts, 43 George III, c.1

AN

A C T

FOR

Dividing, Allotting, and Inclosing the Open Fields, Meadows, Pastures, Commonable and Waste Lands, in the Parish of *Widmerpool*, in the County of *Nottingham*.

WHEREAS there are within the Parish of *Widmerpool*, Preamble. in the County of *Nottingham*, several Open Fields, Meadows, Pastures, Commonable and Waste Lands, containing in the Whole by Estimation One Thousand Eight Hundred Acres or thereabouts:

And whereas the Right Honourable *Charles* Viscount *Newark* is Lord of the Manor of *Widmerpool* aforesaid, and entitled to the Right of Soil of and in the said Waste Lands within the said Manor:

And whereas the said *Charles* Viscount *Newark* is Patron of the Rectory of *Widmerpool* aforesaid, and *Langley Gace*, Clerk, is the present Rector or Incumbent thereof, and entitled to all the Tythes and Tenths, both Great and Small, of or issuing from the Lands and Grounds hereby intended to be divided, allotted, and inclosed, and the present inclosed Lands and Grounds within the said Parish of *Widmerpool* (subject and liable to the Payment of Tythes) or to Modusses or Small Payments in lieu of some Part of the said Tythes:

A   And

but their weight as historical judgements is quite different. The statement about Widmerpool has the merit of being much closer to the experience of individual identifiable human beings but the disadvantage of not telling us anything about even neighbouring villages. The wider statement sums up the experience of a great many people over a long period but does not inform us about anyone in particular.

25 Margaret Clifford, countess of Cumberland

Margaret Clifford (1560-1616) founded Beamsley hospital near Skipton in Yorkshire for 13 poor women under letters patent of 1593. The building was completed after her death by her daughter Anne, who wrote of her mother that 'Shee was of a greate naturall witt and judgment, of a swete disposition, truly religious and virtuous, and indowed with a large share of those 4 morall virtues, Prudence, Justice, Fortitude, and Temperance.'
BL Add. MS 30161, f.3v

A good national history of inclosure will refer to Widmerpool or other places in order to show how real people were affected. A good local history of the inclosure of Widmerpool will show that what happened there was part of a national pattern, not a wholly unique experience.

It is therefore mistaken to regard local history as a junior partner or an easy option. H. P. R. Finberg, the first head of the department of English local history at Leicester University (itself the first such department in an English university), was able to claim that local history, in its fullest sense as the entire history of a particular place, is a higher branch of historical studies than national history. A thorough treatment of one place over the full course of its history requires a knowledge of national developments over a large range of topics and the whole of English history. Although beginners need not start on such a broad front they certainly have to keep the national picture in mind for whatever topic they choose.

Many of the topics which are most attractive to new local historians are ones in which the national dimension is self-evidently to the fore. Social history in the 19th and 20th centuries is a good example. Local historians are interested in education, health care, and the treatment of poverty because they connect directly with the fabric of modern life in England and because there are abundant and easily used sources in local record offices and libraries. The importance of national history to those topics is readily apparent. They were profoundly affected by economic, technical, and social developments which took place countrywide, and by initiatives at a national level, whether by government or other agencies. In fact they are prime examples of local studies where the historian has to look both outwards at national history and inwards at the longer-term development of a particular place.

National themes in particular places

Some of the ways in which national and local history connect in such a topic can be explored by looking at the history of poverty and its treatment. Care for the poor in the Middle Ages and early modern period took place independently of state intervention, but that does not mean to say that only local factors were involved. There was what can be called a national (or international) consensus that Christians had the responsibility to feed and clothe the poor according to their means. How that consensus was expressed depended on purely local factors such as whether there was a religious house and how wealthy it was, or, after the dissolution of the monasteries, whether individuals had the wealth and inclination to endow an almshouse (**25**). The incidence of poverty, as at all times subsequently, was determined both by the nature of the local social and economic system and by trends at a national level. It is impossible to generalise about which factor predominated at different times.

From the 16th century, responses to poverty were determined at least in part by government intervention. Both the old poor law of the Elizabethan period, which operated throughout the 17th and 18th centuries and into the 19th, and the new poor law which replaced it in 1834 were the result of deliberate government acts which had the effect of creating a new framework for poor relief throughout the country. The historian of poverty in a particular area will therefore be concerned to identify how far local circumstances differed within a broadly similar national picture: the causes and extent of poverty locally, how the institutions which were provided on a national basis operated in a particular place, and how successful they were in dealing with the local problem (26, PLATE 3).

The change in the poor law in 1834 which, among other things, shifted the burden of care from individual parishes to unions of parishes, is a classic example of change from above effected by a political decision followed by an Act of Parliament which imposed uniform conditions nationwide. Local historians take as a given set of facts the provisions of the Act: how the new arrangements for raising and spending money operated, how the new poor-law guardians were elected and ran the affairs of their union, and so on. It is not part of their task to be concerned, for example, with the Act's drafting or passage through parliament, though subsequent political reactions to its operation may have a local aspect.

The background to the intervention of the state through the 1834 Poor Law Amendment Act, by contrast, is an area where the local and national perspective must be taken together. The enormous distress of the years during and after the Napoleonic Wars, which exposed the inadequacies of the old poor law, was caused by economic trends whose causes were national (such as poor harvests and high food prices), but whose incidence varied greatly from place to place with local circumstances such as the opportunities for work and the effectiveness of local efforts at relief. In assessing the causes of poverty, the local historian has a positive contribution to make to the national picture.

The particularity of causes in an individual location can be illustrated by looking at a single place, Ormskirk, the market town for the corn-growing and market gardening district of south-west Lancashire. A recent local study by Audrey Coney has shown the very special circumstances of local poverty in the 1840s, stemming from an enormous influx of destitute Irish, who were driven from their own country by famine in the early 1840s and poured into Ormskirk through Liverpool, partly because of a well-established pattern of migratory Irish workers going to the town for harvest work. The overcrowding, poverty, and disease in Ormskirk in the 1840s were unspeakably bad. The condition of the poor in Ormskirk at that time cannot be understood without reference to the national scene. The way that the new poor law operated, economic conditions in the

(42)

64

A STATEMENT SHEWING
THE MAINTENANCE OF EACH PAUPER
In the Workhouse, Moor-Street, Ormskirk,

From *17 Dec. 1835* to *19 March* 183*6*

The Bacon used belongs to the House.

Py flour s

				£	s.	d.	£	s.	d.
Bread Flour	10 Packs at	*23/*	℔ Pack	11	10	8			
Wheat Flour	Packs at		℔ Pack						
Oatmeal	2 Loads at	*26/*	℔ Load..	2	12	—			
Rice	*3 cwt.* lbs. at	*2 4/*	℔ lb.	3	12	—			
Beef	*135 ½* lbs. at	*5 ½*	℔ lb.	3	11	1½			
Potatoes	*95—80* Bushels at	*2 0*	℔ Bushel....	7	19	9½			
Milk	....			6	19	7½			
Salt	....				4	—			
Cheese	....			6	6				
Tea *8/*	Sugar *5/*	Treacle *1/3*		17	3				
Pepper *1/*	Mustard *6*			1	6				
Oil(s) *Soap 18/*	*Candles 5/6*			1	3	6			
Onion *Turf* *Herring 4/*					9	6			
Butter	....			2	4				
Barm	....			6	10½				
Worsted				7					
Coals & Carting	—			5	15	—	48	7	9

42 being the Average Number for 13 weeks,
at *20/4* ℔ Week................................ 46 1 4½

2 Master and Mistress each, for 13 weeks
at *20/4* ℔ Week........................ 2 3 10½

add under the Average............ — 2 6 48 7 9

OPPOSITE

26 Ormskirk workhouse
Ormskirk in Lancashire was unusual
in having two workhouses in the 18th
and early 19th century. One was
used by a group of 14 townships and
parishes in south-west Lancashire.
The other, in Moor Street, had been
acquired under an agreement of 1734
between Ormskirk and 17 other
townships and parishes. Both workhouses passed to the Ormskirk poor-
law union set up in 1837, which used
the one in Moor Street until selling
it and building a larger one elsewhere
in 1853.
BL Add. MS 36876, f.64

country as a whole in the 1840s, and the type of housing likely to be
available to newcomers are all matters on which Mrs Coney rightly
consulted standard textbooks and specialist works. Any future
national historian returning to the question of poverty in the 1840s
will have to take account of her findings in Ormskirk alongside those
from other particular towns. On the other hand, the motive for the
study of Ormskirk and the justification for the piece of research was
to make better sense of the history of that particular place, to see the
problems of the 1840s as one step in the development of an individual
town which can be accounted for as part of a continuing history.

Many local historians begin with an interest in how some national
event or process has affected one community. The range of possible
factors that can be studied locally in such a way is very wide indeed.
It covers individual happenings of fairly short duration, such as a war
or an election campaign; changes which, though short-term in themselves, brought about a new set of economic or social circumstances,
such as the dissolution of the monasteries, the inclosure of open fields
and commons (PLATE 5), or the building of new roads, canals, or
railways; and more broadly conceived themes such as the rise of
industrial society or the decline of the isolated rural community. All
of those themes and others are well covered in books which deal with
the country as a whole. Among the many options open to local
historians, which will differ greatly from place to place, two can be
selected which are often chosen for local study and which illustrate the
pitfalls in examining the operation of a national theme at local level.

The impact of both World Wars on particular towns or villages is
a good subject for local historians because there are useful general
accounts like J. M. Winter's *The Great War and the British People* and
copious, largely untapped local sources, notably local newspapers,
ephemera, and eye-witnesses. The effects of either war on a town or
village could be examined, however, without giving even the remotest
flavour of local life. Finding out which regiments recruited locally,
where bombs fell, and where air-raid shelters were placed is not
enough. It may show how life in general was affected by the experience of war but not how it affected life in a particular place or what
distinguished that place from others. The impact of both wars differed greatly from place to place according to a variety of local circumstances. To take only one example: the 'Pals' battalions formed
by volunteers in many towns and cities during the early months of
the First World War can be understood only by taking a local
perspective. Industrial towns and cities, where men worked together
in large groups, provided proportionately more recruits than rural
areas. The local battalions mirrored the economic structure of the
towns in which they were formed: in the Lancashire cotton town of
Accrington the Pals were workmates from the weaving sheds and factories, whereas in Liverpool groups of lower middle-class clerks from
the offices of the great shipping and insurance companies volunteered

together. The danger of writing about places as if they had no individuality distinct from that of other places is one which applies to social history generally.

Another attractive subject is local transport history. No less than with war, the local historian of transport must be aware of the wider national picture – for instance the general growth of the canal system when writing about a particular canal. The danger here is not of failing to be local enough but of being too local and especially too detailed. From the local historian's point of view, what is interesting about a canal is not the fine detail of its planning, construction, and use but its impact on a particular locality through which it passed. The local historian should look at the canal in context, not in isolation.

Narrowly defined local topics such as the experience of war or the impact of a canal, if approached with local historical questions in mind rather than treated in an antiquarian way, or as a sample of national social life, are not to be disparaged as second-rate local history, mere crumbs from the larger cake of national history which neither satisfy in themselves nor give a reasonable idea of what the cake as a whole is like. English social and economic history, and even in certain respects English political history, is not a Madeira of even consistency throughout but a rich plum pudding with different experiences in every part.

At any of the four levels of local history described in preceding chapters it is important to be aware of comparisons and contrasts with other families, other villages, other towns, and other regions in England. With the type of family history advocated in Chapter One comparisons come automatically. Regional history is partly a matter of balancing the similarities and dissimilarities among different places in order to judge the characteristics of a regional society or indeed to discover where the geographical bounds of that society are to be drawn. For the parish or urban historian, however, it is easy to lose sight of what is typical or exceptional within the story of one particular place. The local historian needs on the one hand to know enough national history to be able to assess the typicality of local circumstances, and on the other to remain sceptical of what national historians have said. Local historians are always finding out new things which refine received wisdom about English history or even contradict it outright.

BURSTEADS : INTERIOR OF GREAT BARN

The Victoria County History, properly 'The Victoria History of the Counties of England' but known to its users by the initials VCH, is by any standards a remarkable enterprise. No other country in the world has produced anything like an attempt at an encyclopaedic local history, and in most the documentary sources for the history of individual places would simply not allow it to be done.

The inclusion of the name 'Victoria' in the title derives from the permission given by Queen Victoria to dedicate the project to her. The VCH is therefore neither a history of Victorian England nor a history of the Australian state of Victoria, as the uninitiated

27 The Victoria County History
The reference set of volumes kept in
the General Editor's office at the Institute of Historical Research, University of London.
Photograph 1988

sometimes think. By 1989 it had published 200 volumes (**27**) to a plan
which has retained essentially the same objective as first set out in
1899. The aim has always been to write an outline local history of
the whole of England, county by county and place by place.

What is meant by local history has changed greatly since the
VCH began work, and the VCH itself has gone through fundamental
changes in its organisation, finance, and staffing, besides its approach
to the subject. It early established itself as a byword for high scholarly
standards and is still the place of first resort for local historians in
England. The very first thing that a local historian ought to know
about a place is whether it is covered in the VCH.

History

Three main phases in the history of the History can be distinguished,
with turning points in its fortunes downwards in 1914 and upwards
in 1947. Both changes were mainly due to the financing of the project;
there was continuity in personnel, location, and organisation between
the different phases, and of aims and methods throughout.

In the first phase, 1899 to 1914, the VCH was a history for
gentlemen largely researched by ladies. The people who were interested in local history in the late 19th century were drawn almost
exclusively from the leisured upper-middle and upper classes of
society. The way that all local history was written therefore catered
for their interests in genealogy, heraldry, and antiquities. Natural
history had not yet fully separated itself: local societies were commonly for 'archaeology and natural history', and the early volumes

28 Advertising the VCH

Although the VCH had some generous private benefactors in its early days, it depended heavily on selling the volumes. This advertising sheet of about 1904 leaves little unclaimed in its appeal to patriotic Englishmen with an interest in history and genealogy. The claim under heading 6 has not been borne out, however, since all the early volumes were still in print in 1935, and many which afterwards went out of print were later reissued in facsimile. In 1989 over 160 of the 200 published were available.

VCH Archives, Prospectuses

These volumes make a personal appeal to every Englishman

THE VICTORIA HISTORY OF THE COUNTIES OF ENGLAND

SEVEN POINTS OF INTEREST

1.

THE VICTORIA HISTORY OF THE COUNTIES OF ENGLAND is one of the *greatest works ever attempted*, in extent, interest and importance, and the largest enterprise of its kind ever undertaken by private effort.

2.

Owing to the thoroughness of the work, it is safe to say that it is a definite finality in English local History, and that *its value will not diminish* as new generations are born to live in the land of their forefathers.

3.

The Editorial Staff and Contributors number many hundreds of *England's finest scholars*.

4.

There is *no Englishman* to whom it does not in some one or other of its features make a direct appeal.

5.

It will be the standard for all time, and also the nearest thing possible to supplying each Englishman with *a history of his own individual ancestors* and of his native land.

6.

It is a treasure for every English home and generation, unprocurable in years to come.

7.

The name of every subscriber for a complete County received whilst the work is in progress will *be printed in the last volume of that County*, making a permanent record.

No family name, no parish is there which has not its special interest for some living person.

of the VCH contain chapters on the flora and fauna of each county.

The VCH was conceived by a publisher as a commercial proposition, backed by some private sponsorship (**28**). A limited company was formed to run it, shares were issued, and subscribers were promised that their names would be included in the last volume of each county set. For obvious reasons, as many counties as possible were started at once.

The First World War brought an end to the first frenetic burst of activity, with nine counties written and either published or ready for publication. The staff dispersed to serve their country in ways other than by writing its local history. Post-war conditions were not favourable. Publishing had become much more expensive and the country house and parsonage market for local history had collapsed. By 1920 the limited company was insolvent and the editor, William Page, was working without a salary. In its second phase, 1914 to 1947, such volumes of the VCH as appeared were produced almost single-handedly by Page and his successor L. F. Salzman. Page, who had taken on the burden of ownership, gave the History to the University of London's Institute of Historical Research shortly before he died in 1933. The University continues to own the VCH and the Institute to manage it.

In its third phase, from 1947 to the present day, the VCH has been written by academically trained professionals for all who are interested in English local history. The scale and productivity of the VCH have expanded, the plan of the project as a whole has been revised to modernise the contents of parish histories, and on average two or three volumes have been published every year since the mid 1950s. In 1947, three counties were being written by the editor with some part-time assistance, Warwickshire, Cambridgeshire, and Sussex. The first has since been completed. From 1947 onwards ten other counties have begun work, financed largely by the generous contributions of local authorities and some other local sponsors in partnership with the Institute of Historical Research. Cambridgeshire and Sussex have both continued with local financial help. The normal arrangement is that county or district councils and others provide funds to employ one or more staff (usually two or three), whose work is published by the Institute.

Contents

As originally planned in 1899, the VCH was not merely a new and larger-scale local history on the model of the many county histories already in existence, even though it shared many of their features and preoccupations. In order to understand what sort of information to expect from the earlier volumes of the VCH, and indeed how the plan has evolved, it is necessary to compare the main features of the 'old style' and the 'new style' VCH with those of earlier county histories.

Until the VCH, individual county histories had normally grown by accretion and re-edition over the years. Thomas Helsby's history of Cheshire published in 1882, for example, was an extension of George Ormerod's history of Cheshire published in 1819, reprinting Ormerod's text exactly as he had written it, bringing the information up to date and making corrections by means of comments in square brackets (**29**). Ormerod in turn had used material collected by earlier historians of the county and indeed reprinted two 17th-century

29 Ormerod's *History of Cheshire*
George Ormerod concluded his account of Monks Coppenhall township in 1817 with a statement about the recent purchase and inheritance of the manor. By 1880, when Thomas Helsby was revising Ormerod's work, the rural township had been transformed into the railway town of Crewe (the station being in the adjoining township of that name). The history of Crewe as a new town is a fascinating story. Helsby confined himself to a brief gazetteer-like description.
BL Printed Books, L.R.262.f.1, vol.3, p.329

The said manor subsequently passed to the Cholmondeleys of Cholmondeley ; and having been purchased from the present marquis by the late Mrs. Anne Elcock of Poole, is now (1817) under her will the property of her nephew William Massey, esq. [in whose family the same appears to be still vested. The chief land proprietors · here, however, are the London and North-Western Railway Company, Edleston's Trustees, and James Atkinson, esq.

Monks Coppenhall, since the introduction of railways, and the construction of the London and North-Western Company's line passing through it from Chester to London, has risen from a village into a populous town in consequence of very extensive engine factories, railway carriage, and other works having been established here by that Company, who are in fact the founders of the town. It is now well known throughout the country as CREWE, but comprises only a small part of Crewe proper, the whole of Monks Coppenhall, and part of Church Coppenhall. It possesses a first-class station, through which an enormous passenger and goods' traffic proceeds to nearly every part of the kingdom. The growth of the town has been rapid during the last quarter of a century, but perhaps more so during the last ten years. Three or four years since, it had a population of 22,000, with an increase at the rate of nearly 2,000 a year. It was constituted a borough in 1877, and is now governed by a mayor and corporation.

accounts. The second important feature of county histories was that they were mostly divided into a general history of the county at large and individual parish histories. The general account often dealt mainly with military and political history. Parish histories covered little more than the history of manors and 'antiquities' (typically parish churches, charities, Roman and earlier remains). There might be a description of present-day communications and industries, but no attempt to treat them historically.

The early VCH did not break the mould of English local history — the framework of counties and parishes within which manorial history occupied the central place — but it did enlarge it and introduce a number of new features. Archaeology, economic history, and religious history (as opposed to churches as antiquities) were brought systematically into local history for almost the first time, though they were treated in general articles covering a county as a whole and not as part of parish histories. A reader interested in a particular place

30 Problems at the Public Record Office
The early VCH undertook large-scale systematic research in the Legal Search Room at the Public Record Office in Chancery Lane. Between 1902 and 1904 the number of requisitions for documents increased by 50 per cent, a large part of which may have been due to the VCH. In 1904, the Secretary of the PRO, S. R. Scargill-Bird, wrote to the editor of the VCH, William Page, to complain about VCH use of the Search Room. Page acceded to his request that numbers be reduced.
VCH Archives, A 30, General 5

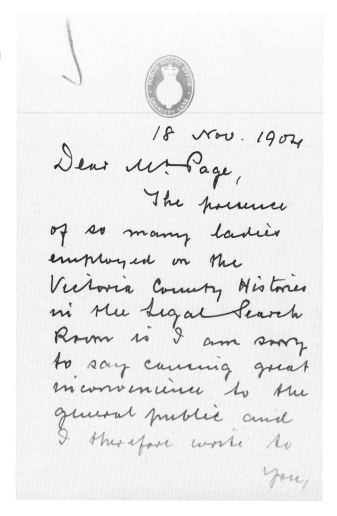

was expected to read the parish history in the light of what was said elsewhere about the history of the county. That remains true of parish histories today despite the wider range of subjects which they now cover.

On the organisational side, the main innovations of the VCH were that it was uniform between counties, that research was methodical and from original sources, and that full references were given so that readers could check the origin of statements and follow them up. The VCH was also unusual in being a cooperative venture. By 1914 a team of almost 50 people was led by William Page as general editor and included architectural advisers mounted on bicycles (Page had wanted motorbikes). Most of the staff before the First World War were young ladies from good families who had read for degrees at Oxford or Cambridge and for whom other opportunities for employment were limited. The more adept among them were allowed to write parish

you, privately in the first instance, to ask whether you can reduce the number to more practicable limits. The Round Room is already overcrowded and I am afraid it is impossible to find other accommodation for

for them.

Yours very truly

S R Scargill Bird

Wm Page Esq. F.S.A.

histories, and some went on from their apprenticeship at the VCH to become well-known historians. Most, however, toiled at extracting references from documents in the Public Record Office and elsewhere for others to turn into parish histories. At times they were so numerous that relations with the staff of the Public Record Office became strained (**30**).

The history of manors long remained at the heart of the VCH approach to local history, particularly in the years after 1914 when most of the general history of the counties had been completed and attention was focused on parish histories. As late as 1944 an academic committee charged with reviewing the role of the VCH regarded its main purpose as 'the accurate registration of the manorial descents which form the central thread of English social history.'* From about 1950, however, the old scheme for writing parish histories was amended to include subjects which had not previously been covered

*Quoted in *VCH General Introduction* (London, 1970) p.23.

and to deal more systematically with others which had been treated
haphazardly or only in general articles. Economic and social history,
the history of population, landscape, and the physical growth of
settlement, elementary education, religious nonconformity, and local
government were all treated place by place.

Throughout its existence the VCH has therefore included two
types of article, 'general' and 'topographical'. In the general volumes
certain topics are dealt with in articles covering the county as a whole.
The great majority of all the intended general volumes have been
published, many of them before 1914. The information in such
articles, which were usually written by an authority in the field, is
often still of great value. For many general subjects, the VCH
achieved almost comprehensive national coverage. Domesday Book,
for instance, is translated with an introduction for all relevant counties
except Gloucestershire (which is forthcoming), Lincolnshire (which
was published elsewhere), and Westmorland; the religious houses of
every county are covered except for Cornwall, Devon, Herefordshire,
Northumberland, and Westmorland; industries were described
historically in all counties but for Cheshire, Devon, Herefordshire,
Huntingdonshire, Norfolk, Northumberland, and Westmorland.

Despite the importance of the general articles in setting local
history on new courses, it is the topographical articles, dealing with
each county systematically place by place, which are rightly seen as
the core of the VCH. Given the enormous changes in the nature of
local history during the 20th century, it is not surprising that parish
histories have become longer and more complex, and have come to
use a much wider variety of sources to deal with a greater number
of topics.

What is perhaps more surprising is that the VCH should have
stuck by the original county and parochial framework. The plan
drawn up at the outset has not been modified in its essentials. The
parishes within each county are dealt with in their 'hundreds', the
second tier of local government below the county from the 10th until
the 19th century. Hundreds have now passed completely out of use
as administrative units. They remain in use by the VCH partly
because they were much longer-lasting than any subsequent local
government units and partly because no better means of dividing
counties into manageable volume-sized sections can be devised.

The territorial units whose histories the VCH writes are parishes.
In the early days the boundaries and framework of 'ancient parishes'
were adhered to strictly, using as a base line the pattern before any
great changes began to be made in the 1880s. Thus, the important
Lancashire town of St Helens, which was not an ancient parish, was
covered in only one and half pages under the subheading 'Borough'
in the account of the township of Windle in the parish of Prescot.
When the social and economic history of the town during the
Industrial Revolution came to be properly written in the 1950s by

T. C. Barker and J. R. Harris, it filled a book of 500 pages. In 'new style' VCH volumes published since the mid 1950s, the parochial framework in rural areas has been formed by civil parishes, the successors of ancient parishes in some cases and of townships in others. Wherever boundaries have been altered, the fact is mentioned and the area being discussed in a parish history is defined. Large towns are dealt with as a whole and since the 1960s outlying rural parishes built over in the 19th and 20th centuries have usually been treated in the same volume.

The contents of a typical parish history (if there is such a thing) have been very different under the old and new schemes. Those published before about 1950 had a thorough account of the manor, church, advowson (the right to appoint clergy), and charities, and some less systematic information about landscape, communications, and economic history. The architecture of manor houses and parish churches was treated in detail. Rufford in Lancashire has many of the most common characteristics. The parish took up just over 12 pages, of which five and a half were occupied by the manor, two by the church and advowson, and three by photographs of the Old Hall and New Hall. The introduction to the history of Rufford did little more than mention the change in its status from township to separate parish and briefly describe the appearance of the landscape and village. The descent of the manor was given in detail with enormous footnotes providing references and a great deal of further information about members of the family. The long description of the Old Hall included a plan. The church was described more briefly, the descent of the advowson was traced, and an incomplete list was given of curates and rectors. The parish charities were mentioned separately.

The 'new style' parish histories which have been written since the 1950s normally have seven or eight sections besides an introduction: Manors and Other Estates; Economic History; Local Government; Church; Nonconformity (or, if appropriate, two sections: Roman Catholicism and Protestant Nonconformity); Education; and Charities for the Poor. The introduction covers, among other topics, population, physical growth, landscape, and social life and institutions. Footnotes are confined to references. Anywhere with a history more complex than that of an ordinary rural parish is treated appropriately. Madeley in Shropshire, technically an ordinary parish but actually including the important industrial settlements of Coalbrookdale, Coalport, and Ironbridge, was written with the additional headings of Communications; Growth of Settlement; Social and Cultural Activities; Agriculture; Mills; Coal and Ironstone; Iron and Steel; Other Metal and Engineering Trades; Quarries and Sandpits; Clay and Ceramic Industries; Markets and Fairs; and Public Services.

The aims which VCH authors must bear in mind when writing the standard sections have been defined in a series of memoranda written for staff use. Thus, for example, the Manors section of a

```
                    V.C.H. CAMBRIDGESHIRE X

        PARISH CHECK-LIST OF NON-P.R.O. MS. &c. SOURCES


British Library

   Main Reading Room

      General catalogue, including blue pages; microfiche
          catalogue for recent accessions.

   Map Room

      General catalogue of printed maps.

   Manuscript Students' Room

      Index of MSS. in B.L. (to 1950)

      Cat. of Additions to MSS. 1951--5

      MS. catalogues of Add. Ch.

      Index to Cole MSS.

      Index to Baker MSS. (including those at Cambridge)

      Add. MS. 5861.  Ely consistory court wills, early 16th
          century (indexes of places in MS.)

      Add. MS. 9412--13.  Lysons's correspondence on Cambs.
          (compare with xerox from published edn.)

      Add. MS. 9465.  Lysons's church notes, alphabetical
          order

      Add. MS. 9822.  Ely priory register (for appropriate
          parishes)

      Add. MS. 15672.  Minutes on ejections, 1644
          (references from Walker Revised, ed. A. G.
          Matthews, giving page nos.)

      Add. MS. 41612.  Ely priory register 1273--1366 (for
          appropriate parishes)

      Cott. MS. Tib. B. ii.  Survey of bishop of Ely's lands
          1222 (for appropriate parishes)

      Cott. MS. Claud. C. xi.  Survey of bishop of Ely's
          lands 1251 (for appropriate parishes)

      Eg. MS. 3407.  Ely priory cartulary (for appropriate
          parishes)
```

31 A VCH checklist
The Cambridgeshire checklists were revised in 1988 when work was about to begin on the final volume of the county set. The first page, shown here, lists various catalogues and indexes in three departments of the British Library, besides certain specified manuscripts. The former are to be searched for items relating to the 26 parishes to be covered in the volume. At this stage, references will be noted down on a slip of paper for each parish, ready to be used as research is undertaken parish by parish.
VCH

parish history 'should mention each lord or owner who is named in the records or may be presumed from them, and should indicate when the land passed from one to another, and whether by grant, inheritance, settlement, or whatever other means', while under Economic History, 'The aim is not to provide a complete history of agriculture in each parish, but to sketch the main agricultural features within the history of the parish'.

Towns and cities are dealt with at much greater length than rural parishes. The history of Oxford, published in 1979 in a volume of over 500 pages, is an example, though treatment differs according to circumstances. The history of Oxford University had been covered in an earlier volume. About half of the Oxford city volume is taken up with a general account of the city's history from its origins to the 1980s in three chronological chapters. They cover economic history, the development of the town, local government, relations with the university, and social and religious life, among other things. The second half of the book gives a more detailed account of various aspects of Oxford's history, buildings, and institutions, some of the headings being: Boundaries; Communications; Castle; Markets and Fairs; Craft Guilds; Mills and Fisheries; Municipal Buildings; Parish Government and Poor Relief; Public Services; Sites and Remains of Religious Houses; Churches; Roman Catholicism; Protestant Nonconformity and Other Christian Bodies; Non-Christian Religious Bodies; Social and Cultural Activities; Education; Charities for the Poor; and Street-Names.

The local history of London has always been a particular problem for the VCH's county- and parish-based framework. One general volume, dealing with the City of London's religious history, was published in 1909. The history of the metropolis outside the City has otherwise been, or is to be, dealt with as part of Kent, Middlesex, Surrey, and Essex. Of the counties which contributed successively to the territory of the London County Council between 1889 and 1965 and to the London boroughs after 1965, the small area of southern Hertfordshire was completed by the VCH in 1923 before any of it was transferred administratively to London, while Kent has had no topographical volumes published. VCH Surrey was completed before 1914 and shares the unsatisfactory aspects of other urban areas treated under the old scheme. Essex's topographical volumes, published since 1956, have covered all the London boroughs and include a general article on 'Metropolitan Essex'. The Middlesex VCH has written the history of all the parishes of what has been termed 'Outer Middlesex' (*ie* that part of the county left outside the LCC) and is now making its way through 'Inner Middlesex' (the former LCC area which stretches from Hammersmith and Hampstead in the west to Hackney and Poplar in the east). The problem of how to write the history of the City of London, which has the most complicated and best documented history of any place in England, has not yet been confronted.

Methods

The present research practices of the VCH are no less systematic than those of the early days. The main problem to be overcome has been to take into account the much greater amount of source material that has become available, for example through accumulation in county record offices and better indexing in the Public Record Office, without the time spent on an individual parish stretching towards infinity. One of the most effective means of controlling the number of sources searched, while ensuring that nothing essential is omitted, has been the preparation of checklists of manuscript and printed sources for each county (31). The items to be gone through systematically for every parish range from items as specific as 'Tax. Eccl.' (the printed edition of the papal taxation of ecclesiastical revenues in 1291 which lists churches and their values) to those as general as 'place name index at county record office'. The first might take a minute to locate in a library and note the information for an individual place; the latter could well produce hundreds of documents for a single parish which might take weeks to work through. Some sources are examined for all the parishes in a volume or in a whole county at one time.

VCH authors are encouraged to make their notes in a uniform way on standard-sized slips of paper incorporating the name of the parish in the top right corner and including an accurate reference to the source from which the information has been copied. The method of using slips was adopted right at the start of the VCH's existence and indeed when a new parish is begun the author will normally find that

32 An old VCH 'slip'
The 'feet of fines' at the Public Record Office (class CP 25) were searched systematically by the VCH ladies in the early days. A 'fine' or final concord normally records a sale of freehold property, in this case at Burwell, Cambridgeshire, from John and Elizabeth Edward to Theodore and Mary Goodwyn in 1600. The document was written out in triplicate on one sheet of parchment, for the buyer, the seller, and, across the foot, as a copy kept by the court of Common Pleas.
VCH

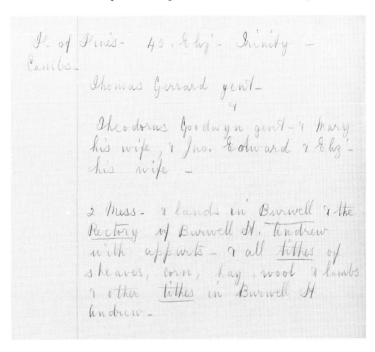

TOP

33 Research
A member of the VCH staff at work
in the Students' Room of the British
Library Department of Manuscripts.
The manuscript is one of Christo-
pher Towneley's volumes of tran-
scripts of Lancashire deeds (2).
Photograph 1988

BOTTOM

**34 Using a computer in the VCH
offices at the Institute of
Historical Research**
Photograph 1988

a small quantity of 'old slips' already exists, in the neat handwriting
of well-educated young ladies of the 1900s and 1910s (**32**).

Most of the counties in progress have microcomputers which are
used for word-processing the text of parish histories and increasingly
for storing and processing data as it is collected (**34**). The day is not
far distant when staff will be equipped with lap-top computers to take
into record offices and input notes from sources directly.

Coverage

The VCH's coverage of the country is inevitably patchy. Of the 39
ancient English counties, 11, and one of the ridings of Yorkshire, have
been completed. Of them, all but Warwickshire were written entirely
under the 'old scheme' and mostly before 1914. Twelve counties were
in progress in 1989. The extent of their completeness ranged from
Cambridgeshire, where work began in 1988 on the final volume, and
Cheshire, which by 1989 had published three general volumes. The
only topographical volumes outside the counties completed and in
progress are one for County Durham, two for Leicestershire, and two
with part of a third for Northamptonshire. Eleven counties and the
West Riding thus have only between one and three general volumes
to their credit, while Northumberland and Westmorland have none
at all. The 200 volumes published up to the middle of 1989 are sum-
marised in the appendix (*see* p.76).

What VCH authors write in parish histories, and have in mind as
they gather material in libraries and record offices (**33**), is an introduction to the history of a particular place. The account of any place must
record systematically the main features of its history: the fluctuations
in population, the succession of principal landowners, how the inhabitants have made a living and in doing so altered the environment
around them, how they have worshipped and how their life as a community has evolved over hundreds of years. It must draw attention
to what is different and what is typical about that one place in relation
to its neighbours, to wider regions, and to the country at large. It must
be a store of references for the national historian who may be interested in the career of only one landowner or the growing of a single
crop, but satisfying for the local historian who is a native or resident
of the place. It must be accurate in every respect. What the VCH
publishes about the history of any particular place can never be the
last word. It is an outline, a starting point for other local historians,
and an introduction to one small corner of the local history of
England.

DUNSTABLE PRIORY

Getting started on the history of a house

There are two basic sources for the history of any house: the building itself and maps. The appearance of a house is the most important clue, notably whether it is constructed of modern mass-produced materials like standard bricks and clay tiles or traditional local materials, normally showing a date before the mid 19th century. Maps should be consulted early on, especially Ordnance Survey maps at a library and manuscript maps from the early 19th century and before at the local record office. There may be other clues in the character of the district and in street names. Once the possible date of a house is narrowed down, a more detailed search can begin in street directories, rate books, and more specialised sources.

Sometimes, a house of rather ordinary appearance has an unusual history. No 13 Belmont Road is the middle house in a terrace of three in Ironbridge, Shropshire, built of bricks with a tile roof (**a**). From the outside it looked like a typical early 19th-century house, but a map of 1847 showed a much larger building labelled 'workhouse' occupying its site (**b**). Some specific questions could therefore be posed. When did the workhouse close? Was it completely demolished or is the terrace part of it? When was the workhouse built?

The fact that a workhouse was involved meant that the search began with the minute books and correspondence of the Board of Guardians for Madeley poor-law union. They showed that the Guardians took over the building shortly after 1834 from the earlier poor-law authority, the overseers of Madeley parish. The Guardians extended and altered the building several times before selling it in 1874 when a new workhouse was built elsewhere. What happened to it afterwards was established in outline by looking at the house again more closely. Most of the workhouse buildings had been demolished and their foundations were discovered in the garden. The rooms at the front and the back of the terrace had entirely different proportions and brickwork, the construction of the back rooms being consistent with a date about 1874 whereas those at the front were certainly earlier and probably belonged to a workhouse building divided into three by inserting new walls and doorways. Turning therefore to the records of the Madeley overseers, it was found that the original building was put up as a 'house of industry' for the parish about 1796, a date which fitted the building work at the front.

In 1989 further research on its history was still in progress, including a closer inspection of the building itself, searching for other maps and documents, especially plans of the workhouse known to have been made at the time of the 19th-century extensions, and investigating its more recent history by talking to the last owner, who had lived there since the 1930s.

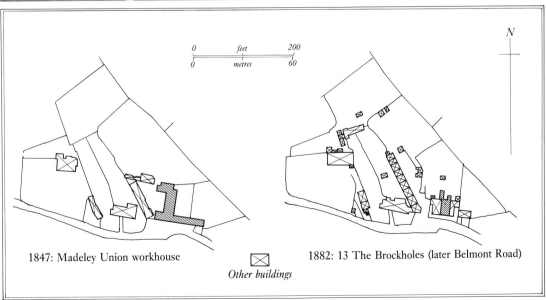

1847: Madeley Union workhouse

Other buildings

1882: 13 The Brockholes (later Belmont Road)

Getting started on the history of a school

c Log book of Harrow Green School, Leyton
Waltham Forest Archives, L 58.71/1, pp.224-5

None of the numerous and varied sources for the history of an individual school makes a better starting point than its log books. Head teachers of government-assisted schools were legally required to keep a log book as a daily record. They are highly miscellaneous compilations, dealing indiscriminately with assistant teachers, pupils, parents, and government inspectors, and varying in tone as much as the characters of the headmasters who wrote them. Log books are often accompanied by attendance registers, letter books, school photographs, and other documents which contribute to a picture of daily school life. Many have been deposited in local record offices, the first place to inquire for their existence and whereabouts. Some are still kept at the school or a successor, or at the offices of the local education authority.

The headmaster of Harrow Green School in the east London suburb of Leyton between 1884 and 1910 was A. P. Wire, clearly an ebullient character whose log books are full of fascinating detail about his school. A number of particular episodes stand out among the daily

d Prizewinners, Harrow Green
School, 1908
Waltham Forest Archives, L 58.71,
negative no.12190

routine, especially a school strike in 1889 (**c**). Wire was an enthusiastic
photographer and the log books also record the lantern slide shows
which he gave to his pupils. A collection of his photographs has been
kept with the log books. They show outings in Wanstead Park, school
sports, and playground games. Even the posed shots of school
prizewinners have a delightful informality which brings the school to
life (**d**).

Log books, attendance registers, and photographs show vividly
what a school was like but do not tell its history. A very brief account
of all the schools in Leyton is given in volume 6 of the Victoria
County History for Essex. Harrow Green School was opened by the
Leyton school board under the 1870 Education Act in 1877 and closed
down in 1935. It held 1200 pupils after 1882. To fill out its history,
or for a school not covered by the VCH, it will be necessary to search
through parliamentary papers and other printed sources in a major
public library, and the original records of the Department of Education in the Public Record Office at Kew.

Getting started on the history of a family

e Henry Lewis
Original photograph in possession of
C. P. Lewis

The first two stages of family history normally take place at home and in St Catherine's House in London. The first step is to turn out the loft for old photographs and family papers and ask your older relatives about their parents and grandparents. You should then visit the

CERTIFIED COPY OF AN ENTRY OF MARRIAGE   Given at the GENERAL REGISTER OFFICE, LONDON

Application Number R11860

[Marriage certificate of Edward Lewis and Eliza Parkinson, Registration District of Burnley, marriage solemnized at St Paul's Church in the parish of St Pauls, Burnley, in the Counties of Burnley and Lancaster, 2 April 1892]

f Modern copy of a marriage certificate of Edward Lewis and Eliza Parkinson, issued by General Register Office
In possession of C. P. Lewis

General Register Office, St Catherine's House, 10 Kingsway, London WC2, to look at the indexes of births, marriages, and deaths since 1837 and to order, for a fee, the actual certificates. Begin with the earliest known marriage or birth and search backwards for alternate births and marriages.

One of the old photographs owned by my own relatives was of an old man who they said was my grandfather's grandfather, who had died aged 91 about 1932 (e). No one knew his first name or where he had originally come from. The search therefore had to start nearer the present. I knew from family information that his grandson (my grandfather) was born in 1898 in Burnley, the son of Edward Lewis and Eliza Parkinson. Searching the marriage indexes backwards from 1898 revealed matching entries in the second quarter of 1892 for an Edward Lewis and an Eliza Parkinson. The certificate gave Edward's father's name as Henry Lewis and his occupation as blacksmith (f). Since Edward was aged 23 when he married on 2 April 1892, he must have been born between 3 April 1868 and 2 April 1869 and I was able to find his birth certificate, from which I got the names of both parents. That led to their marriage certificate. By then I knew a lot more about the old man in the photograph. Henry Lewis, whose father John was an engine driver, was 21 when he married Isabella Wiseman of Burnley on 6 February 1864. A blacksmith, he was living at Cononley in the West Riding of Yorkshire. The couple were married nearby at Skipton Register Office. Later I found from a directory of Burnley that he was still a blacksmith between 1893 and 1908, and also where he lived then. So far, however, I have not found his family in the censuses of 1861, 1871, or 1881, or his birth certificate. Burnley is dauntingly big to search through the censuses systematically and my ancestor could be any one of the numerous Henry Lewises whose births were registered in 1842-3.

Getting started on the history of a village

yearly. There is a reading room, known as the Cottenham Philo-Union, well supplied with the principal daily and weekly papers. There is also a coffee and reading-room, opened February 1881. A handsome pavilion has been erected on the recreation ground which is so arranged that it can be flooded during a severe frost and used for skating The old road from Belsar's Hills to Aldreth High Bridge runs along a corner of the parish: it was the old British road out of the Isle of Ely. The old Carr Dyke runs across the fens; and close to it, on the boundary next Landbeach, many remains of Roman pottery have been found; a beautiful bronze bust was discovered there in 1855. This village was formerly noted for the superior quality of its cheese, which article, some years ago, was produced here in large quantities, but latterly the extensive pastures have been converted into arable land. The fruit gardens are extensive and increasing; and hundreds of tons of fruit are sent during the season to London, Manchester, and other markets. There are six manors—viz. Crowlands, Lyles, Sames, Burdley or Harlston, Rectory manor and Pelhams.

Board School.—In 1864 a British school was erected at a cost of about £1,000; it is now leased to the School Board, who also erected additional schools at a cost of £1,550, to hold 500 boys & girls; a large piece of land has also been purchased as a playground; Alfred Goddard, master; Miss Ellen Beard, mistress; Miss Collins, infants' mistress

A Free school was endowed by Catherine Pepys, for 16 boys; the present schoolhouse was built out of the funds belonging to the Moreton's Charity. This school is now closed, & a scheme is in contemplation whereby the funds accruing from this Charity shall be distributed in scholarships & rewards to children attending the Board School

A Sunday & night school is held in a school-room, built by the late rector, adjoining the rectory

CARRIERS.—James Chapman, to 'Old Red Lion,' Cambridge, wed. & sat.; Daniel Payne, to Granby, tues. & sat.; Jonathan Chivers, to Pickerel, Cambridge, tues. thurs. & sat. 8 a.m. returning same days

PRIVATE RESIDENTS.

Arber Mrs
Barker Rev. Frederick M.A. Rectory
Birkett Mrs
Bridger John
Chambers Robert
Cox Charles Hayden, The Limes
Cross Mrs. Betsy
Cross Norman
Cross Thomas
Cross Mrs. Sarah
Egerton Rev. John B.A. [curate]
Emerson Mrs. Oliver
Few Misses
Goode Mrs
Graves James, Milford house
Hall Thomas Ivatt, Manor house
Harris Ernest
Ivatt Mrs. Frances
Ivatt George
Ivatt Mrs. John
Ivatt Robert Martin, Gothic house
Ivatt Mrs. Susan
Ivatt Thomas, Dunstall house
Ivatt Mrs. William
Jones Rev. Alfred Emlyn [Baptist]
Kempton William
Male Arthur James
Moore William, Euston house
Norman Miss Eliza
Norman Mrs

Smith John Graves
Smith Joseph
Todd John, London cottage
Towers Mrs. Euston house
Watson Charles
Watson Mrs. Ebenezer
Watts Mrs. Frances
Watts Mrs. John

COMMERCIAL.

Ainger William, farmer
Bartingale John, farmer
Bartingale John, jun. Black Horse
Beecher James, farm bailiff to William Peed esq
Bennett Edward, harness maker
Benton Thomas, farmer
Bicheno William & Son, farriers
Bolton Alfred Joshua, Lord Nelson, & coal merchant
Bridger John, surgeon, & med. off. & pub. vacc. 7th dist. Chesterton Union
Bull Arthur, farmer
Bull William Chivers, farmer
Burgess John, plumber
Butler Henry, boot & shoe maker
Chambers Ann (Miss), fancy repository
Chapman James, market gardener
Chivers Charlotte (Mrs.), mineral water maker
Chivers Ebenezer, brewer & farmer,

Cottenham Gas Company Limited (Richard Haird, sec)
Cottenham Philo-Union (Frederick Cross, sec)
Cox Charles, beer retailer
Cox Chas. Hayden, surgeon, The Limes
Cox James, Red Lion
Coxall William Denson, farmer & cattle dealer
Cross Charles, butcher & farmer
Cross Ivatt Osborn, farmer
Cross Jeremiah, farmer
Cross John, farmer
Cross John, shopkeeper
Cross Thomas, jun. farmer
Cross William, grocer & draper
Cross William, market gardener
Dean & Adamson, steam plough proprietors, Victoria house
Diddell Caroline (Mrs.), saddler
Doggett Emma (Mrs.), baker
Ellard Thomas, brazier
Emerson Francis, farmer
Everett John & Son, carpenters
Few John, farmer
Finch James, Fountain, & plumber
Froment William, carpenter
Gantrey & Sons, agricultural seed & fruit growers
Garrett Emanuel, farmer
Gautrey Azariah, shopkeeper

g *Kelly's Directory of Cambridgeshire*
(1883)
BL Printed Books, PP.2505.ybi

The range of possible sources for the history of a village is enormous, but if the right ones are chosen at the outset, quick progress can be made in discovering things about it. It is best to begin with 19th-century sources that are accessible locally, legible, and fairly comprehensive. Directories, census enumerators' books, and large-scale maps are ideal.

From the mid 19th century to the Second World War, directories were published for all English counties at intervals of no more than four or five years. For each village and town there is usually a short description followed by a list of the farmers, tradesmen, and 'private residents'. The entry for the large village of Cottenham from *Kelly's Directory of Cambridgeshire* for 1883 (g) gives some idea of the character of that particular village: farmers and market gardeners were very numerous and there was a wide range of shopkeepers and tradesmen and many well-to-do private residents. There were evidently some local occupational dynasties, such as the market gardening Gautrey family.

The census enumerators' books for 1851, 1861, 1871, and 1881 list

Page 18]

The undermentioned Houses are situate within the Boundaries of the

Civil Parish [or Township] of	City or Municipal Borough of	Municipal Ward of	Parliamentary Borough of	Town or Village or Hamlet of	Urban Sanitary District of	Rural Sanitary District of	Ecclesiastical Parish or District of
Cottenham						Chesterton	

No. of Schedule	ROAD, STREET, &c., and No. or NAME of HOUSE	HOUSES Inhabited (U.), or Building (B.)	NAME and Surname of each Person	RELATION to Head of Family	CONDITION as to Marriage	AGE last Birthday of Males	AGE last Birthday of Females	Rank, Profession, or OCCUPATION	WHERE BORN	If (1) Deaf-and-Dumb (2) Blind (3) Imbecile or Idiot (4) Lunatic
84	Wesleyan Villa High Street	1	Charles Ditton Newman	Head	Mar	30		Wesleyan Minister of Cottenham Chapel	Surrey Ditton	
			Sarah Ann Newman	Wife	Mar		37		Bristol	
			Amy Eliza Do	Daur	—		12	Scholar	London	
			Arthur Harold Do	Son		11		"	Lincolnshire Boston	
			Edith Mary Do	Daur			9	"	"	
			Ernest Henry Do	Son		7		"	Kent Tunbridge	
			Ethel May Do	Daur			4	"	Isle of Wight Ventnor	
			Gertrude Annie Do	Daur			1		Cambs. Cottenham	
			Elsie Louisa Do	Daur			2mo		" Bristol	
			Elizabeth Biddle Silcox	Sis in law	Unm		40		Cambs. Bampton	
			Caroline Barnes	Serv	Unm		X	House-maid	Suffolk Mildenhall	
			Jane Sheldrick	Serv	Unm		15	Nurse-maid		
85	"do.	1	William Gautrey	Head	Mar	42		Gardener of 8 acres	Cambs. Cottenham	
			Sarah Do	Wife	Mar		43		Over	
			Robert Do	Son	Unm	17		Gardener	Cottenham	
			Emma Do	Daur			13	Scholar	" "	
			Mina Jane Do	Daur			12		" "	
			Ada Mary Do	Daur			10		" "	
			Arthur Wm Do	Son		8			" "	
			Edwin Do	Daur			4		" "	
			Arthur Harry Do	Son		2			" "	
86	do	1	James Chivers	Head	Mar	58		Ag. Labourer	" "	
			Mary Anne Do	Wife	Mar		52		" "	
			Felicia Do	Daur			14	Scholar	" "	
			Minnie Do	Daur			12	ao	" "	
	Total of Houses..	3		Total of Males and Females..		8	17			

NOTE.—Draw the pen through such of the words of the headings as are inappropriate.

h Census enumerators' book for Cottenham, 1881
Public Record Office, RG 11/1659, f.43v

by household every individual in a village on the night of the census, giving name, marital status, age, sex, relationship to head of household, occupation, and place of birth. That for Cottenham in 1881 can be profitably compared with the 1883 directory (h). Only one of the three households on the census page illustrated appears in the directory, namely that of the gardener William Gautrey. One of his neighbours, James Chivers, was a labourer and so would not be listed in the directory, while the other, the Wesleyan Methodist minister Charles Ditton Newman had probably left the village two years later. Methodist ministers did not stay long in one post, as the birthplaces of the Newmans' children show. (Compare where the children of William Gautrey and James Chivers were born.)

The Ordnance Survey published maps at scales of 6 inches and 25 inches to the mile, the earliest in the 1840s but for some counties not until the 1880s. Those for Cottenham could be consulted to pick out where the Newmans, Gautreys and Chiverses lived in 1881, since we might well expect 'Wesleyan Villa' to be named on a map of that scale.

By using all the available directories, censuses, and maps of Cottenham, a detailed study could be made, for instance, of its occupations and the stability of its resident population at a time when rural villages were changing fast. The same can be done for any village in the country. All three sources should be found (the census books on microfilm) in a combination of local record offices and larger public libraries.

Getting started on the history of population

i Return of households in the diocese
of Ely, 1563
BL Harley MS 594, f.200

One of the most important things to discover about any place is the size of its population and whether it was growing, declining, or remaining steady at different times. A range of sources from Domesday Book in 1086 to the most recent census is available for all placces, but there are difficulties with the pre-19th-century evidence which make it advisable to read a specialist introduction, such as the appropriate chapter in W.B. Stephens, *Sources for English Local History*.

Almost all the sources dating from before 1801 were compiled for a purpose other than simply numbering the people. Taxation records such as the returns of the 1377 poll tax omitted children, those too

County of CAMBRIDGE.

HUNDRED, &c.	PARISH, TOWNSHIP, or Extra-parochial Place.		HOUSES.			PERSONS.		OCCUPATIONS.			TOTAL OF PERSONS.
			Inhabited.	By how many Families occupied.	Uninhabited.	Males.	Females.	Persons chiefly employed in Agriculture	Persons chiefly employed in Trade, Manufactures, or Handicraft.	All other Persons not comprized in the Two preceding Classes.	
CHILFORD - -	Abingdon, Great -	Parish	47	50	—	133	139	219	46	7	272
	Do Little - - -	Parish	34	38	—	99	86	56	14	115	185
	Babraham - - -	Parish	38	50	—	98	98	67	2	127	196
	Bartlow - - -	Parish	13	17	1	38	45	20	2	61	83
	Castle Camps - -	Parish	74	106	1	260	286	157	173	216	546
	Hildersham - -	Parish	26	45	—	79	91	131	18	21	170
	Horseheath - -	Parish	50	74	1	166	176	54	19	269	342
	Linton - - - -	Parish	183	246	—	590	567	170	153	829	1,157
	Pampisford - - -	Parish	35	46	—	100	102	56	5	141	201

j Table of population from the 1801 Census
BL Official Publications Library, Census 1801, Population Abstracts, Enumeration, p.21

poor to pay, and those who managed to evade payment. Ecclesiastical records like the 'Compton census' of 1676 were interested only in adults. Medieval documents often listed households without revealing how many people lived in each. Parish registers can be pressed into service to give an idea of whether population was naturally increasing or falling in the late 16th, 17th, and 18th centuries, but not what its absolute size was at any given moment. Since 1801, the census has given a reliable figure of population on a particular night at intervals of 10 years (except in 1941) but other much less comprehensive evidence must be used to examine trends between censuses.

Sources from different periods and with different purposes are not always comparable, though an attempt can sometimes be made. In 1563, households in every place throughout the country were counted, though the returns survive for only nine dioceses, including Ely (i). If we assume that the numbers represent families, together with any servants who lived with them, the figures can probably safely be compared with the number of families recorded in the 1801 census (j). Of the six parishes which appear in both extracts, Little Abington and Hildersham more than doubled their numbers of families between 1563 and 1801, Great Abington, Babraham, and Pampisford increased by about a third or half, while the number in Bartlow apparently fell. The comparison at least makes a starting point for investigating the differing population histories of the six parishes during the early modern period.

General Introduction	1 vol 1970 + supplement 1989
Bedfordshire	complete; 3 vols + index; 1904-14
Berkshire	complete; 4 vols + index; 1906-27
Buckinghamshire	complete; 4 vols + index; 1905-28
Cambridgeshire	in progress; 9 vols + index; 1938-
Cheshire	in progress; 3 vols; 1979-
Cornwall	1 vol + 2 parts (not indexed*); 1906-24
Cumberland	2 vols (not indexed); 1901-5
Derbyshire	2 vols (not indexed*); 1905-7
Devon	1 vol (not indexed); 1906
Dorset	2 vols; 1908, 1968
Durham	3 vols (not indexed*); 1905-28
Essex	in progress; 10 vols; 1903-7, 1956-
Gloucestershire	in progress; 7 vols; 1907, 1965-
Hampshire	complete; 5 vols + index; 1900-14
Herefordshire	1 vol (not indexed); 1908
Hertfordshire	complete; 4 vols + index; 1902-23
Huntingdonshire	complete; 3 vols + index; 1926-38
Kent	3 vols (not indexed*); 1908-32
Lancashire	complete; 8 vols; 1906-14
Leicestershire	5 vols; 1907, 1954-64
Lincolnshire	1 vol (not indexed); 1906
London (City)	1 vol (not indexed); 1909
Middlesex	in progress; 9 vols; 1911, 1962-
Norfolk	2 vols (not indexed); 1901-6
Northamptonshire	4 vols (not indexed*); 1902-37
Northumberland	no vols
Nottinghamshire	2 vols (not indexed); 1906-10
Oxfordshire	in progress; 11 vols; 1907, 1939-
Rutland	complete; 2 vols + index; 1908-36
Shropshire	in progress; 5 vols; 1908, 1968-
Somerset	in progress; 5 vols; 1906-11, 1974-
Staffordshire	in progress; 9 vols; 1908, 1958-
Suffolk	2 vols (not indexed); 1907-11
Surrey	complete; 4 vols + index; 1902-14
Sussex	in progress; 9 vols + index; 1905-7, 1935-
Warwickshire	complete; 8 vols + index; 1904-8, 1945-69
Westmorland	no vols
Wiltshire	in progress; 14 vols; 1953-
Worcestershire	complete; 4 vols + index; 1901-26
Yorkshire	general vols complete; 3 vols + index; 1907-25
East Riding	in progress; 5 vols; 1969-
North Riding	complete; 2 vols + index; 1914-25
West Riding	no vols
York	complete; 1 vol; 1961

* The translations of Domesday Book are, however, indexed for Cornwall, Derbyshire, Kent, and Northamptonshire, and that of Boldon Book for Durham.

Further Reading

Books about how to study English local history are very numerous. Nevertheless, there are some which are outstandingly useful for beginners. Best of all is Philip Riden's *Local History: a Handbook for Beginners* (London: Batsford, 1983; paperback), which is short and very practical. One particularly good introduction to family history is Stella Colwell's *The Family History Book: a Guide to Tracing Your Ancestors* (Oxford: Phaidon, 1984; paperback), while houses are covered by John H. Harvey in *Sources for the History of Houses* (London: British Records Association, Archives and the User, vol 3, 1974; out of print but available in libraries).

For inspiration in choosing a theme, any one of three well-written and well-illustrated books can be recommended: David Hey, *Family History and Local History in England* (London: Longman, 1987; paperback); the latest edition of W. G. Hoskins, *Local History in England* (London: Longman, 1984; paperback); and Alan Rogers (editor), *Group Projects in Local History* (London: William Dawson, 1979; paperback), which is equally suitable for individuals. David Dymond also has sensible ideas on choosing a subject in *Writing Local History: a Practical Guide* (London: British Association for Local History, 1981; paperback). For more advanced work, the standard guide to sources is W. B. Stephens, *Sources for English Local History* (Cambridge: University Press, 1981). A quarterly journal, *The Local Historian*, and a magazine appearing six times a year, *Local History*, keep readers up to date with news, guides to sources, and reviews of new books.

The particular studies mentioned in the text are listed below:

T. C. Barker and J. R. Harris, *A Merseyside Town in the Industrial Revolution: St Helens 1750-1900* (Liverpool: University Press, 1954).

M. W. Beresford, *Time and Place: an Inaugural Lecture* (Leeds: University Press, 1961) (on Leeds).

John Chandler, *Endless Street: a History of Salisbury and its People* (Salisbury: Hobnob Press, 1983).

C. G. A. Clay, *Economic Expansion and Social Change: England 1500-1700*, 2 vols (Cambridge: University Press, 1984).

Audrey Coney, 'Mid 19th-century Ormskirk: disease, overcrowding and the Irish in a Lancashire market town,' *Transactions of the Historic Society of Lancashire and Cheshire* (forthcoming).

B. J. Davey, *Ashwell 1830-1914: the Decline of a Village Community* (Leicester: Leicester University Department of English Local History, Occasional Papers, 3rd series, vol 5, 1980).

H. J. Dyos, *Victorian Suburb: a Study of the Growth of Camberwell* (Leicester: University Press, 1961).

Alan Everitt, *Continuity and Colonization: the Evolution of Kentish Settlement* (Leicester: University Press, 1986).

Richard Gough, *The History of Myddle*, ed. David Hey (Harmondsworth: Penguin, 1981).

P. D. A. Harvey, *A Medieval Oxfordshire Village: Cuxham, 1240 to 1400* (Oxford: University Press, 1965).

W. G. Hoskins, *The Making of the English Landscape* (Harmondsworth: Penguin, 1985; new edition by Christopher Taylor, London: Hodder, 1988).

W. G. Hoskins, *The Midland Peasant: the Economic and Social History of a Leicestershire Village* (London: Macmillan, 1957).

J.R.Ravensdale, *Liable to Floods: Village Landscapes on the Edge of the Fens, A.D. 450-1850* (Cambridge: University Press, 1974).

A.L.Rowse, *Tudor Cornwall*, new edition (London: Macmillan, 1969).

Margaret Spufford, *Contrasting Communities: English Villagers in the Sixteenth and Seventeenth Centuries* (Cambridge: University Press, 1974).

Joan Thirsk (ed.), *The Agrarian History of England and Wales*, vol 4, *1500-1640* (Cambridge: University Press, 1967).

Flora Thompson, *Lark Rise to Candleford: a Trilogy* (Harmondsworth: Penguin, 1973).

Angus J.L.Winchester, *Landscape and Society in Medieval Cumbria* (Edinburgh: John Donald, 1987).

J.M.Winter, *The Great War and the British People* (London: Macmillan, 1986).

Index